罗 澄　男，毕业于武汉大学，获英语语言与文学专业学士、硕士。后留学加拿大多伦多大学及马尼托巴大学，获得语言学暨应用语言学博士，并任教于加拿大布鲁克大学应用语言学系，为该系终身教授，历任系主任、研究生部主任等职。目前兼任武汉大学珞珈学者暨讲座教授及广西大学的客座教授。

罗澄博士的教学与科研涉猎广泛，包括功能语言学、句法学、语义学、语用学、话语分析学，以及应用语言学中的语言测试学、二语习得、阅读理论、研究方法论等。他在各种国际会议和知名学科杂志上发表、宣读近百篇论文并著有 *Analysis of Typical Errors in English by Chinese EFL Students*；*A Picture is Worth... 1000 Words*；*Beginner Chinese Reader Series* 等专著。还应邀到美国、泰国和多次回国进行学术报告、专题讲座、讲课及其他学术文化交流活动，为传播中华文化和促进中加学术交流与合作作出了重要贡献。

语言学系列丛书

CLEFTABILITY in LANGUAGE

Cheng Luo

语言强调结构研究

罗澄 著

WUHAN UNIVERSITY PRESS
武汉大学出版社

图书在版编目(CIP)数据

语言强调结构研究/罗澄著.—武汉：武汉大学出版社，2009.8
语言学系列丛书
ISBN 978-7-307-07187-2

Ⅰ.语… Ⅱ.罗… Ⅲ.语法结构—研究 Ⅳ.H04

中国版本图书馆 CIP 数据核字(2009)第 123048 号

责任编辑:王春阁 责任校对:王 建 版式设计:詹锦玲

出版发行：武汉大学出版社 (430072 武昌 珞珈山)
(电子邮件：cbs22@whu.edu.cn 网址：www.wdp.com.cn)
印刷：通山金地印务有限公司
开本：720×1000 1/16 印张:12.5 字数:231 千字 插页:3
版次:2009 年 8 月第 1 版 2009 年 8 月第 1 次印刷
ISBN 978-7-307-07187-2/H·657 定价:24.00 元

Contents

List of Tables/Figures

Abbreviations

A(BS)	absolutive
ACC	accusative
AH	the Accessibility Hierarchy
APPL	applicational suffix
ASP	aspect
AUX	auxiliary
B	benefactive
CFM	contrastive focus marker
CH	the Cleftability Hierarchy
COMP	complementizer
CPL	copula
D	dative
dem; DEM	demonstrative (pronoun)
DET	determiner
DETRANS	detransitivizer
DIR	directive
DO	direct object
DO_m	middle clause direct object
DP	declarative particle
E(RG)	ergative
EMPH	emphatic marker
F	feminine
FUT	future (tense)
GEN	genitive NP
INDEF	indefinite
INF	infinitive

INT	interjective
IO	indirect object
LOC	locative
LF	logical form
m	masculine
M	measure word
MM	modifier marker
NEG	negative particle
NOM	nominalizer
NONPST	non-past (tense)
OBL	oblique NP
OComp	object of comparison
OM	object marker
P(L)	plural
PERF	perfective (aspect)
PRES	present (tense)
PRO	pro-form
PROG	progressive (aspect)
PRON	pronoun
PROP	proper noun
PRT	particle
PST	past (tense)
RC	relative clause
REL	relative marker
RESULT.	resultative
RM	relative marker
S	sentence
S(G)	singular
SBJN	subjunctive (mood)
SU	subject
TRANS	transitivizer
vi.	intransitive verb
VN	verbal noun
vt.	transitive verb

†	grammatical but a little odd
?	marginally grammatical
? *	problematic
*	ungrammatical

Preface

Research in language universals as anchored in functional linguistics has drawn continued attention and interest from linguists, language educators and professionals of other applied linguistics areas in recent years. Through studying crosslinguistic variation, important generalizations about natural languages can be made which would not be revealed by investigating any single language. In that regard, previous studies of the Noun Phrase Accessibility Hierarchy as a universal tendency have largely focused on relativization, whereas those of cleft sentences have barely touched upon cleftability with regard to the Accessibility Hierarchy. Given such a gap in the research, it seems that a systematic crosslinguistic investigation of cleftability with regard to the Accessibility Hierarchy will add significant contribution not only to the research on cleft construction by converging the Accessibility Hierarchy studies and the research on cleft sentences, but also to finding out how human languages avail themselves of various linguistic strategies for contrastive emphasis in communication in the study of language universals as an important part of linguistic theory.

The present monograph is such an attempt. Furthermore, since clefting differs from relativization in that it affects not only NPs but also non-NPs, an adequate account of cleftability will have to go beyond the scope of the Accessibility Hierarchy, to accommodate cleftability of non-NP as well as NP constituents. A principal goal of this book, therefore, is to develop a principled account for cleftability in general.

The general organization of the book is as follows:

Chapter 1 is a general introduction, which identifies the research problem and its significance, provides the necessary theoretical background through literature review, and discusses the theoretical issues and methodological specifics involved.

Chapter 2 deals with NP cleftability. After an initial proposition of a Cleftability

Hierarchy, a Continuity Constraint, and a set of criteria for measuring cleftability, data from various languages will be examined and analyzed against each of the criteria as well as the Continuity Constraint, to attest the proposed Cleftability Hierarchy.

Chapter 3 continues to examine NP cleftability in terms of some apparent counterevidence found in some languages. Closer scrutiny of two kinds of such counterexamples, pattern incongruence of cleftability hierarchy in ergative languages and uncleftability of direct object in Chinese, reveals the interactive nature of the Cleftability Hierarchy in relation to typological features of a language and to some language specific constraints.

Chapter 4 examines non-NP cleftability. Through analysis of cleftability of PPs, ADVPs, APs and VPs, a nouniness principle will be advanced to account for cleftability of non-NPs as well as NPs. Evaluation of this principle with regard to its descriptivity will be made toward the end of the chapter.

Chapter 5 reviews strengths and weaknesses of both the Cleftability Hierarchy and the Nouniness Principle, and proposes a unified, discourse-functional explanation for cleftability in general. Empirical evidence will be presented in support of such an explanation, presented as the Thematicity Principle.

Chapter 6 adds an important dimension to the typology of cleft sentences, with special reference to the contrastive focus marker. Though not directly related to the issue of cleftability, some interesting research findings regarding the use of focus markers, deictic pronouns and copulas will be presented, findings that support a functional-iconic view of language.

To facilitate the readership's understanding of crosslinguistic data, all crosslinguistic examples are presented phonetically, with both morpheme-by-morpheme glossing and free translation. For Chinese data, both phonetic and character representations are given. Finally, a language index and a subject index are provided at the end of the book for ease of reference.

In preparing this monograph, I owe much to my mentor and one of the prominent contemporary linguists, John Haiman, whose philosophical thought of and rigorously scientific approach to linguistic study have left visible marks on this work. I am also grateful to Terry Russel, John Nichols and Pat Mathews for their helpful feedback during the early stages of this project, to James Tai, whose work in and approach to Chinese linguistics had inspired part of the present study, and to Moshe Nahir for his valuable advice on Hebrew. Special thanks go to Wuhan University Press and my long-time colleague Chunge Wang, whose support is indispensable in publishing this book. Finally, the completion of this monograph was in part funded through a Wuhan University Luojia Fellowship, for which I am deeply appreciative.

by Cheng Luo

Chapter 1 Introduction

1.1 The Noun Phrase Accessibility Hierarchy

Studies of crosslinguistic variation can often lead to important generalizations about natural languages, generalizations that can not be reached by investigating any single language. For instance, consistent general patterns of crosslinguistic variation in certain syntactic constructions can be characterized by a number of grammatical hierarchies in typology. A classical example is Keenan and Comrie's (1977) crosslinguistic study of relative constructions, which vary from language to language both in relativizing strategies and in noun phrase (NP) positions available for relativization, but which follow a general pattern in terms of relativizability. This general pattern, known as the Noun Phrase Accessibility Hierarchy (henceforth AH), aims to account for the relativizable NP argument positions across languages, by virtue of an implicational scale for the relativizability of different grammatical functions. By comparing relative clauses in fifty odd languages, Keenan & Comrie (1977) argue for the existence of the Noun Phrase Accessibility Hierarchy as in (1), where the positions toward the left are claimed to be universally more accessible for relativization than those toward the right.

(1) The Noun Phrase Accessibility Hierarchy

SU > DO > IO > OBL > GEN > OCOMP

In (1), SU stands for subject; DO, direct object; IO, indirect object; OBL, oblique NPs such as those headed by prepositions or postpositions; GEN, possessive NPs; and OComp, object of comparison, such as the post-*than* NP in English.

According to the Noun Phrase Accessibility Hierarchy, subjects are more accessible to, or easier for, relativization than direct objects, which are more accessible to relativization than indirect objects, which in turn are easier to relativize than any lower position, and so on. Since subject is the easiest position to relativize, any language that has a relativizing strategy can relativize on subjects, any language that can relativize on direct objects can also relativize on subjects, and so on down the Hierarchy (Maxwell 1979).

The proposed Noun Phrase Accessibility Hierarchy is subject to a working principle known as the Continuity Constraint, expressed here as (2):

(2) The Continuity Constraint

Any relative clause-forming strategy must apply to a continuous segment of the AH; and strategies that apply at any one point of the AH may in principle cease to apply at any lower point. (Keenan & Comrie 1977: 67)

Thus some languages have relative clause (RC) forming strategies which apply only to subjects, for example, the Western Austronesian language Toba Batak (Keenan & Comrie 1977); other languages have strategies which apply only to subjects and direct objects, for example, Persian (*ibid.*), and still other languages have ones which apply only to the top three positions on the Accessibility Hierarchy, for example, Tamil, etc. (*ibid.*). But no language, it is claimed, could relativize, say, direct objects and oblique NPs in the same way unless it can also relativize indirect objects in that way. In other words, (1) and (2) can be expressed as a set of implicational universals in the following sense: given a certain strategy, if a language can relativize, for example, direct objects, then it can relativize subjects; if a language can relativize indirect objects, then it can relativize direct objects and subjects; and so forth. Thus, a grammatical hierarchy like the AH covers a chain of implicational universals, such that the implicatum of the first universal is the implican of the second, the implicatum of the second universal is the implican of the third, and so on. Put together, the chain can be summarized as: if an NP on the AH is accessible to relativization in a language, then all NPs higher on the hierarchy are also accessible to the same process. Generalizations like this, as claimed by Keenan (1987), determine constraints on the form and substance of possible human languages.

The proposed Accessibility Hierachy has so far been claimed to gain a fair measure of validity as a language universal in a number of psycholinguistic and text studies, notably Keenan & Hawkins (1987), although exceptions and problems are not lacking (Keenan & Comrie 1977, 1979; Maxwell 1979; Stenson 1979; Sigurd 1989; Fox 1987; Comrie 1981, chap. 7; and Lehmann 1986); and various attempts (e. g. Cole et al. 1977; Fox 1987; Tallerman 1990) have been made to either modify it with different versions of extension or interpret it from different perspectives.

In addition to relativization, other syntactic processes have also been studied with regard to the AH. For example, Johnson (1974) and Trithart (1975) argue that operations which promote NPs low on the AH to higher positions, as via passivization, distribute according to the AH. Thus, if a language can promote locatives to subjects (e. g. *The forest was seen-in e a lion by John*), then it can necessarily promote indirect objects and direct objects to subjects as well (e. g. *Mary was shown the picture by John*).

1.2 The Cleftability Hierarchy

From the above discussion, one would be tempted to extend the applicability of the Accessibility Hierarchy to other syntactic processes, such as clefting, given its close structural and functional resemblance to relativization (Schachter 1973). However, in spite of the bulk of existing literature on the Accessibility Hierarchy, little systematic study on clefting has been known to provide evidence that the AH is, or to what extent it is, applicable to clefting crosslinguistically in terms of cleftability of various grammatical positions. Studies of the AH have largely been with regard to relativization, with little if any reference to clefting. On the other hand, studies of cleft sentences, though abounding, have barely touched upon cleftability with regard to the AH in any systematic way. Most research concerning the cleft construction has centred on its appropriate underlying structure and its derivation, for example simplex derivation (e. g. Jespersen 1949; Ennaji & Sadiqi 1986), pseudo-cleft derivation (e. g. Akmajian 1970; Gundel 1977; Bolinger 1972; Chafe 1976); copula sentence derivation (e. g. Wirth 1978; Heggie 1988), base generation (e. g. Delahunty 1984; Knowles 1986; Hedberg 2000), and dual-source analysis (e. g. Hankamer 1974; Pinkham & Hankamer 1975). Other studies have focused on the semantics and/or pragmatics of cleft sentences (e. g. Declerck 1984; Halvorsen 1976; Prince 1978; Horn 1981; Collins 1987). Few, if any, have dealt with cleftability; and even among the few which do, such as Declerck's (1983, 1984) study on cleftability of English adjective phrases (APs) and Collins' (1987, 1991) quantitative text study on English clefted constituents, none have been associated with the Accessibility Hierarchy in a crosslinguistic perspective. Given such a gap in the research, it seems that a systematic crosslinguistic investigation of cleftability with regard to the AH will add significant contribution not only to the research on cleft construction by converging the AH studies and the cleftability studies, but also to finding out how human languages avail themselves of various linguistic strategies for contrastive emphasis in communication in the study of language universals as an important part of linguistic theory.

The present monograph is such an attempt. Furthermore, since clefting differs from relativization or passivization in that it affects not only NPs but also non-NPs, an adequate account of cleftability will have to go beyond the scope of the AH, to accommodate cleftability of non-NP as well as NP constituents. A principal goal of this book, therefore, is to develop a principled account for cleftability in general.

The book attempts to answer the following questions:

A. Does NP cleftability crosslinguistically conform to the Cleftability Hierarchy, (3), which is hypothesized on the basis of the Accessibility Hierarchy, (1)?

(3) **The Cleftability Hierarchy**

SU > DO > IO > OBL > GEN > OComp

B. What principle(s) govern(s) the cleftability of various kinds of non-NPs, supposing they show different degrees of cleftability from NPs?

C. Is there a general principle which provides a unified account for NP and non-NP cleftability? If so, what is it?

(3) deals mainly with NP clefts. Question A, then, involves NP clefting; and Question B involves non-NP clefting. As the discussion evolves, it will be seen how the two aspects interact with each other, yielding a unified account of cleftability in general. Before we take up these questions, however, it is necessary to first address some theoretical and methodological preliminaries related to the study of clefting and cleftability.

1.3 Theory and Methodology

1.3.1 AH as a universal tendency

Hawkins (1988) classifies universals into three major types: absolute universals, implicational universals, and distributional universals. Absolute universals define linguistic characteristics found in all languages, as those claimed in the Universal Grammar by Chomskyan linguists. Implicational universals stipulate limitations on language variation, defining possible and impossible combinations of characteristics, as do the Greenbergian universals. Finally, distributional universals define frequency scales or hierarchies, in terms of degrees of structural complexity of various kinds, markedness, degrees of processing difficulty, and interplay between different principles. Both implicational and distributional universals are scalar, or tendencies, rather than absolute. The Accessibility Hierarchy in question, while possessing some properties of implicational universals analytically, as mentioned in 1.1, is as a whole some kind of distributional universal, in the sense that it is related, in one way or another, to structural complexity, intralinguistic and crosslinguistic frequency of occurrence, and degrees of markedness, all of which may eventually be accounted for in terms of processing difficulties. All of these aspects will be addressed with respect to a set of criteria proposed for measuring cleftability.

1.3.2 A working definition of *clefts*

1.3.2.1 Previous definitions

One of the methodological concerns is the definition of clefts. At first sight, the problem seems nonexistent, given some readily available classical definitions such as Jespersen's (1961):

(4) A cleaving of a sentence by means of *it is* (often followed by a relative pronoun or connective) serves to single out one particular element of the sentence and very often, by directing attention to it and bringing it, as it were, into focus, to mark a contrast.

(4) defines cleft sentences both structurally and functionally. However, definitions like this are directed only toward the description of languages like English, and may either miss some universal definitive features of the said construction or overgeneralize language-specific features. For example, Lee (1963), Chomsky (1970), Akmajian (1970) and Bach and Peters (1968) all posit a sentence-initial *it* in the underlying structure of the cleft sentence. *It* plays a prominent role in these analyses, which are based on data from English alone. However, from a broader crosslinguistic perspective, this expletive *it* is only a grammatical phenomenon specific to some verb-second (V2) languages like English, but does not exist in many of the world's languages. Therefore, the expletive *it* may not necessarily be present in the underlying structure of the cleft sentence from a crosslinguistic perspective. In this sense, definitions like (4) lack generality as a more universal definition needed in

crosslinguistic studies of cleft sentences.

As an alternative, consider Teng's (1979: 101) definition:

(5) A cleft sentence is a construction where a particular sentential constituent is marked by means of a syntactic or a morphological device for the purpose of focus, contrast or emphasis.

Compared with (4), (5) is more general in that it defines cleft sentences in more languages and may well serve as a more universal definition of clefts. However, a closer scrutiny reveals that (5) does not properly exclude the so-called pseudo-clefts such as "What he saw was a bear" (cf. "It was a bear that he saw."), which also meet the definition①. With all the similarities between clefts and pseudo-clefts (Akmajian 1970), there are a number of important structural as well as functional properties which distinguish between them (Prince 1978; Delahunty 1984, Collins 1987, 1991; Dik 1985; Givón 1990). It is only reasonable, therefore, to define clefts distinctly from pseudo-clefts.

1.3.2.2 Clefts in non-configurational languages

A second concern in defining clefts has to do with non-configurational languages. It has been observed that many of the world's languages, unlike most Indo-European languages, are non-configurational and, as such, do not exhibit overt structural dependency between two positions in constructions such as WH-questions and cleft sentences. It is claimed that WH-questions and cleft sentences in such languages do not involve any dislocation. For example, in forming a cleft sentence, such a language will not formally dichotomize a sentence into focus and presupposition by dislocating the highlighted constituent. Thus, consider Chinese②

(6) a. Zhang San zuotian lai le.
Zhang San yesterday come PERF
"Zhang San came yesterday."
张三昨天来了。

b. *Shi* *Zhang San* zuotian lai de.
CFM Zhang San yesterday come MM

---

① For further discussion on contrast, focus and emphasis, see Declerck (1984).

② All through this book, I use the term "Chinese" to refer to Mandarin which is widely recognized as the standard version of modern Chinese. Since the focus of the study is not phonological or phonetic in nature, no possible confusion with other Chinese dialects will arise.

"It is Zhang San who came yesterday."
是张三昨天来的。

c. Zhang San *shi* *zuotian* lai de.
Zhang San CFM yesterday come MM
"It is yesterday that Zhang San came."
张三是昨天来的。

(6a) is a non-cleft sentence. In (6b-c), the foci are marked by the contrastive focus marker (hence CFM), *shi*, and the focused constituents remain in the same position as in the corresponding non-cleft sentences.① No dislocation is apparent in the structure. Many other unrelated languages, such as the Dravidian language Malayalam (Mohanan 1982, cited in Andrews 1985), and the Chadic language Margi (Hoffmann 1963), also exhibit a similar structure.

Cleft sentences of this kind prompt the question as to whether the term "cleft" is justifiable when used to describe sentences like (6b-c), or the term *contrastive focus sentence* is descriptively more appropriate. The answer to the question lies in two considerations: (i) Is it true that no dislocation of any kind is involved in such cases? (ii) Does the term *contrastive focus sentence* correctly define all, and only, sentences like (6b-c)?

The answer to (ii) is quite straightforward. The term *contrastive focus* applies to at least four kinds of constructions:

a. stress/tone focus sentences (e. g. Igbo (Robinson 1972))
b. clefts (of the English kind)
c. pseudo-clefts
d. non-configurational clefts (as in (6b-c))

All these sentence types have a contrastive focus and can be described with the term *contrastive focus sentence*. Therefore, to use the term will not clearly distinguish among the different types of contrastive focus constructions. For this reason, the term "contrastive focus sentence" is considered as, at least at this point, no more enlightening than "cleft".

For question (i), Huang (1982a) has offered possible clues to an answer.

---

① The Chinese cleft sentence is also often marked by the modifier marker (MM) toward the end of the sentence (Ross 1983). However, as Teng (1979) points out, this marker is not always needed.

While arguing for universality of the Subjacency Condition, Huang shows that, like WH-questions, cleft formation in Chinese, though not involving overt movement, has to obey Subjacency, just as relativization and topicalization do:

(7) * wo xihuan *shi* *Zhang San*$_i$ [$_{NP}$[$_S$ e_i mai de] nei-zhi gou]
I like CFM Zhang San buy MM that-M dog
"* I like the dog that it is Zhang San that bought."
我喜欢是张三买的那只狗。

(7) shows the impossibility of focusing a constituent inside a complex NP, an instance of Ross' (1967) Complex NP Constraint, which Chomsky (1981) incorporates into the Subjacency Condition. Clefts in Chinese, therefore, show properties as *if* they obey Subjacency. A non-movement analysis, according to Huang, would not only fail to account for the ungrammaticality of (7), but, more seriously, pose a serious problem for the "proposed putative universal condition" in the theory. As a solution, an LF rule, Focus (= Move-α), is proposed which, operating in Logical Form (LF), moves the focused constituent into the highest COMP in (7) and violates the Subjacency Condition. Thus ungrammaticality of (7) is accounted for. It is concluded (Huang 1982a) that languages like Chinese do involve Move-α at an abstract level of LF, motivated by both Universal Grammar and language-specific properties.

If we accept the above argument, then the use of the term "cleft" to describe sentences like (6) seems to be justified, since they involve some kind of dislocation, though not overtly. However, two problems need to be addressed. Theoretically, Huang's whole argument seems to be based on the assumption that Subjacency is a constraint on transformations, i. e. on movement or deletion. In other words, if a language has sentences that obey Subjacency, they must have involved movement in some way, either in SS or in LF. However, as Cole *et al* (1977) cites James (1972), island constraints are not necessarily restricted to movement or deletion; they also apply where no movement or deletion is involved. An example is the exclamation *ah* in English, which cannot occur in islands such as sentential subjects, complex NPs or coordinate structures, to express surprise in respect of the proposition reported. Consider James' example (cited in Cole *et al*. 1977: 28):

(8) a. Ah, it is reported by *Newsweek* that Kissinger is a vegetarian!
b. Ah, that Kissinger is a vegetarian is reported by *Newsweek*!

In (8a), which has an extraposed sentential subject, *ah* can express surprise with regard to the fact that *Newsweek* made the report, or with regard to the content of the report. In (8b), which involves the island-forming sentential subject, only the former interpretation is possible. In other words, the syntactic insertion of *ah* as an expression of surprise over the content which is syntactically embedded in the sentential subject is subject to Subjacency, i. e. the effect of the exclamation cannot penetrate into the island. The theoretical issue here is that Subjacency may not necessarily be transformation-bound. Therefore, examples like (8) cast some doubt on the validity of Huang's argument along the following line: if Subjacency applies to both movement and non-movement rules, then it would be logically flawed to say that a cleft sentence in which no overt dislocation has occurred must involve movement in LF simply because it obeys Subjacency. The LF rule Focus, then, is not well supported until this theoretical problem is resolved.

Empirically, we note that the relativized NP in (7) is the direct object of the matrix sentence. If Subjacency applies, (9a), where the relative clause is part of the subject of the matrix sentence, would be ruled out. But this is in fact not the case.

(9) a. *shi* *Zhang* *San*$_i$ [$_{NP}$[$_S$ $\underline{e}_i$ mai de] nei-zhi gou] pao le.
CFM Zhang San buy MM that-M dog ran = away PERF
" * It is Zhang San who bought that dog ran away. "
是张三买的那只狗跑了。

b. [*shi* [*Zhang San mai de* *nei-zhi gou*]] pao le.
CFM Zhang San buy MM that-M dog ran = away PERF
"It is the dog that Zhang San bought that ran away. "
是张三买的那只狗跑了。

c. *shi* *Zhang Sani er-bu-shi* *Li Si* [$_{NP}$[$_S$ $\underline{e}_i$ mai de] nei-zhi gou] pao le.
CFM Zhang San but-not-CFMLi Si buy MM that-M dog ran = away PERF
" * The dog that it is Zhang San but not Li Si who bought ran away. "
是张三而不是李四买的那只狗跑了。

One may argue that (9a) is grammatical because it is ambiguous between (9a) and (9b), and it is the reading (9b) that makes the sentence grammatical. However, consider (9c), where the contrast clearly rules out a reading like (9b) but the sentence is still grammatical. In fact, a simple change of word order in (7), represented as (7b) here, yields a much improved, if not fully grammatical, sentence.

(7) b. ? *shi* *Zhang San* mai de nei-zhi gou wo xihuan
CFM Zhang San buy MM that-M dog I like
" * The dog that it is Zhang San that bought I like."
? 是张三买的那只狗我喜欢。

In (7b), (9a) and (9c), Subjacency would be violated by Huang's analysis, but no ungrammaticality results. Thus, Subjacency fails to account for these sentences. Given the subject-object asymmetry noted in (7b) and (9a), it seems that the ungrammaticality of (7) results not so much from Subjacency as from word order constraints in Chinese (see 3.2 for a detailed discussion of such a constraint). In any event, for a rule of LF movement to hold, it has to properly account for the above cases.

On the other hand, sentences like (6b-c) do present a semantico-pragmatic dichotomy between focus and presupposition, which is seen contextually from the Chinese example, (10):

(10) A: Zhang San ba beizi da-po le.
Zhang San OM cup break PERF
"Zhang San broke the cup."
张三把杯子打破了。

B: Bu dui. *Shi* *Li* Si da-po de.
not right CFM Li Si break MM
"No, it's Li Si who broke (it)."
不是。是李四打破的。

In (10), Speaker B strongly contrasts Speaker A's view that the person who broke the cup is *Zhang San*, by contrastively focusing on *Li Si*. The fact that someone broke the cup is treated as given/known information which forms the presupposition/background for the asserted. Given such a division, we may consider sentences like (6b-c) as being "clefted" into two parts, with one of the constituents singled out for contrastive focus. As Dik (1980: 225) puts it, this constituent "may remain within the S[entence] in the original position". The same view is expressed in Andrews (1985) where reference is made to Malayalam, a Dravidian language, which has cleft focus marked by morphological suffixation alone, with the focused NP "remain[ing] in its underlying position without being dislocated". (p. 84) Therefore, it seems plausible to recognize such sentences in non-configurational languages as clefts without having to posit abstract movement in

LF as Huang (1982a) does.

Another reason for including sentences like (6b-c) as clefts is the crosslinguistic, typological approach of our investigation. As shown above, many languages, such as Margi and Malayalam, do not have cleft sentences of the English type; however, their semantico-functional equivalents to English clefts do show cleftability patterns similar to those in languages like English. Exclusion of such sentences from consideration will not only result in an incomplete picture about cleftability, but also fail to present an adequate typological description of cleft-like constructions in general, especially considering their conformity to the Cleftability Hierarchy to be discussed in later chapters. It seems, then, that it is desirable to have a definition which is general enough to include cleft or cleft-like sentences in both configurational and non-configurational languages, yet narrow enough to exclude pseudo-clefts and stress-focus sentences from consideration.

1.3.2.3 A working definition

Given what has been considered, (11) will be proposed as a working definition, following Teng (1979) but with some crucial modification:

(11) A cleft sentence is a construction in which a particular constituent is marked by means of a non-equative① syntactic device and/or morphological device for the purpose of focus, contrast, or emphasis.

The syntactic device is predominantly left-dislocation, although some languages also have right-dislocation, and the morphological device is usually some focus marker such as one identical in form with a copula or a pronoun. Most cleft sentences usually have concomitant stress on the focused constituent; however, since phonological devices such as stress are not the focus of this study, they will not be dealt with in detail unless they are crucially related to some morpho-syntactic processes.

As can be seen, (11) can not only accommodate clefts in non-configurational languages, it also properly excludes stress-focus sentences, which are marked by purely prosodic features, and pseudo-clefts with an equative copular construction, which can be attested from the reversibility between the preverbal and the postverbal constituents. According to (11), three types of cleft sentences can be identified in

---

① An equative syntactic device is one like the pseudo-cleft construction, where the pre- and post-copula constituents can be reversed without affecting grammaticality. The term "non-equative" is used here to properly exclude such constructions.

terms of focus-marking devices:

(i) clefts via syntactic means alone, i. e. dislocation or dependency:

Aguacatec (Larsen & Norman 1979)

(12) a. ja Ø-Ø- b'iy yaaj xna'n
ASP 3SA-3SE-hit man woman
"The man hit the woman."

b. *yaaj* m- Ø- b'iy-oon xna'n
man DES. ASP-3SA-hit-DETRANS woman
"It was the man who hit the woman."

As seen in (12), Aguacadec has an unmarked VSO order. What distinguishes between the non-cleft (12a) and the cleft (12b) is the left dislocated cleft focus, *yaaj* "the man", which is followed in (12b) by a clause-like element. Compared with a corresponding English cleft, both the expletive *it* and the copula are absent, and there is no focus marker or complementizer adjacent to the cleft focus. Therefore, it appears that only the syntactic means of dislocation is responsible for marking the cleft construction①. However, this type of clefting is quite rare, probably because of its structural ambiguity with topicalized constructions.

(ii) clefts via morphological means (= focus marker) alone:

Chinese

(13) a. wo zuotian kanjian ta le.
I yesterday see 3s MM
"I saw him yesterday."
我昨天看见他了。

b. wo *shi* *zuotian* kanjian ta de.
I CFM yesterday see 3s MM
"It was yesterday that I saw him."
我是昨天看见他的。

As shown earlier, the only difference between a noncleft (13a) and a cleft (13b) in Chinese is the presence of a contrastive focus marker in (13b), which occurs

① There are some minor morphological changes such as the disappearance of the ergative subject prefix from the verb stem, and the addition of a detransitivizing suffix *-oon*. However, these changes result from clefted ergative NPs (see 3. 1 for details), and do not reflect the general clefting pattern in Aguacadec.

immediately before the cleft focus. Chinese, then, uses only a morphological means to mark a cleft focus.

(iii) clefts via both syntactic and morphological means:

Kpelle (Welmers 1964)

(14) a. Sumo è wɛɛ wúru tèe à yu ǹ i su
Sumo 3s yesterday sticks cut with axe forest inside
"Yesterday Sumo cut sticks in the forest with an axe."

b. *Sumo bé* wɛɛ wúru tèe à yu ǹ i su
Sumo CFM yesterday sticks cut with axe forest inside
"It was Sumo who cut sticks in the forest with an axe yesterday."

c. *wúru bé* Sumo è wɛɛ ˋ-tèe à yu ǹ i su
sticks CFM Sumo 3s yesterday 3s-cut with axe forest inside
"It was sticks that Sumo cut in the forest with an axe yesterday."

The Kpelle data as presented in (14b-c) shows that in Kpelle cleft sentences, as compared with the noncleft (14a), the cleft focus occurs initially and is marked by *bé*, which functions as a contrastive focus marker. Thus, clefting in Kpelle involves both syntactic and morphological means.

1.3.3 Clefting strategies

Like relative clause formation, many natural languages have two or more formally distinct strategies of forming cleft sentences, the most common being deletion and pronoun retention. In (14) above, while (14c) uses a resumptive pronoun prefix '-where the focused constituent has a dependent relationship with a gap in the presupposed clause, (14b) does not employ one. These are identified, respectively, as the pronoun retention strategy and the deletion strategy, which are widely observed in cleft sentences as well as relative clauses of different languages. Put it simply, deletion simply leaves a gap where the focused constituent has been dislocated, and pronoun retention leaves behind a pronominal copy of the dislocated constituent.

According to Keenan's (1972) Principle of Conservation of Logical Structure (CLS), pronoun retention strategy is viewed as a psycholinguistically more facilitating device than deletion in making certain less accessible constructions more accessible. Basically, the CLS holds that the more syntactic structures preserve features of their corresponding logical structures, the more accessible these structures are. In languages in which resumptive pronouns are retained in relativized positions (e.g. Hebrew, Persian and Welsh), relativization is permitted in a greater number of structural configurations, including those intuitively more difficult structures such as islands in Ross (1967) and positions low on the AH (Keenan & Comrie 1977). This is because pronoun retention is only minimally disruptive in terms of case recoverability (Givón 1990).

Likewise, in Jacaltec (Craig 1977), relativization is marked by less and less deletions as we move down the Accessibility Hierarchy. Keenan's argument is that pronoun retention extends the set of relativization environments because relative clauses with retained pronouns correspond more closely to their logical-semantic structures than do relative clauses formed with the deletion strategy. Since the retained pronoun identifies the semantically appropriate position of the NP within the construction that is coreferential to the head, it renders the coreferential relationship semantically more transparent. This in turn makes it easier to understand what the relative clause and the head are being used to refer to. The basis of semantic transparency which underlies Keenan's account of the retention strategy is reiterated in Cole *et al* (1977).

Furthermore, as Hawkins (1988) points out, given what is said in the last paragraph,

> this means that the wider applicability of rules such as RCF [i. e. relative clause formation] in pronoun-retaining languages is not just a function of a more transparent relationship between surface structure and logical structure; it is the result of semantic transparency and process[ing] ease. The comprehension and production of RelCl is facilitated by pronoun retention, and hence certain independent considerations involving real-time language processing reinforce a semantic principle (CLS) in explaining cross-linguistic differences in syntactic rule behaviour.

In this view, the pronoun retention strategy is motivated by both semantic transparency and processing ease.

In terms of clefting, then, it follows that preservation of the logical form in a sentence through pronoun retention helps keep the underlying structure more transparent and facilitates processing, by allowing the cleft rule access to structures which would otherwise be less accessible. Therefore, given two NPs which occupy different positions on the Cleftability Hierarchy, the one that can be clefted via deletion and has less access to pronoun retention is considered more accessible than the one that can be clefted via pronoun retention and has less access to deletion. The rationale of this is the idea of counter-balancing: what is more accessible may occur in more opaque/marked constructions.

Following Keenan & Comrie (1977), I will also hypothesize the following constraint:

(15) Any clefting strategy in natural languages must operate on continuous segments of the Cleftability Hierarchy, and a strategy that applies at any one point on the CH may in principle cease to apply at any lower point.

Hence, if a certain clefting strategy is applied to two NP positions on the Cleftability Hierarchy, it must also be applicable to all intermediate positions as well. For example, presumably, no natural language has a clefting strategy that works only on subjects and oblique NPs but not on direct objects and indirect objects as well.

1.3.4 Other methodological considerations

1.3.4.1 Reduced Cleftability Hierarchy through collapsing

Since the Cleftability Hierarchy only specifies an ordered set of potential grammatical distinctions a language may choose to realize, it is not obligatory that a language realize all the distinctions. Rather, languages are free to choose which distinction(s) they will avail themselves of, but no language is obliged to opt for all the distinctions (Keenan & Gary 1987: 122), i. e. in the majority of cases, a given language does not have enough distinct ways of clefting to justify the particular ordering of *all* the six positions on the Cleftability Hierarchy. Often than not, individual languages tend to show partial structural realizations of the whole set of categorial distinctions of the Cleftability Hierarchy. For example, a language may not have a distinct category *indirect object*, in that all constituents semantically or functionally equivalent to indirect objects in other languages are treated in all respects like objects of prepositions or postpositions, as in Kinyarwanda (Keenan & Gary, 1977). If this is the case, then the Cleftability Hierarchy in that language will simply have the form:

(16) SU > DO > OBL > GEN

But the hierarchy generalizations which are expressed in terms of the Cleftability Hierarchy will remain unchanged in their application to that language. It will still be the case that any given clefting strategy must operate on a continuous segment of the reduced hierarchy, and that if positions low on the hierarchy can be clefted, then so can all intermediate positions. In fact, many languages do collapse the OComp position with the OBL position (e. g. Chinese), and other languages collapse oblique NPs with direct objects①. Therefore, within limits to be determined empirically, particular languages opt for different subsets of the set of categorial distinctions of the Cleftability Hierarchy, and the result is often a reduced hierarchy.

1.3.4.2 Measurement of grammaticality and universality

This study will view grammaticality as being scalar rather than categorical. This is because grammatical rules are not exceptionless laws, but rather leave some fuzzy areas where grammaticality becomes a matter of "more or less" rather than "either... or". In actual use of language, as Givón (1984:12) puts it,

> categories conform to their basic definitions in the majority of cases, and rules obey their strict description more likely than not. But there is always a certain amount of messy residue left, one that does not seem to fit into the category/rule in the strictest sense of their definition.

Therefore, grammatical rules are probabilistic at least in part, and grammaticality in language use may be more appropriately represented as a continuum according to which some sentences may be judged grammatical, some ungrammatical, and some problematic but not completely ruled out depending on context. With such a scalar view of grammaticality, grammaticality will be marked as follows: (i) fully grammatical sentences will be unmarked; (ii) grammatical sentences that sound a little odd will be marked with †; (iii) dubiously grammatical sentences will be marked with ?; (iv) sentences problematic but not completely ruled out will be marked with ?*; and (v) ungrammatical sentences will be marked with *.

By the same token, crosslinguistic generalizations will be regarded as tendencies

① Such cases will be found in languages with serial verb constructions, such as Akan and many other West African languages, as well as Thai, Vietnamese, and a number of other languages of South Asia. In such languages *John killed the chicken with a knife* might be rendered, word for word, as *John used a knife kill the chicken*, and *John brought the book to Bill* as *John takes the book go Bill*. The apparently simplex sentence presents two verbs, both of which occur independently in that form as simple verbs of main clauses.

rather than absolute laws, i. e. they are tendencies that are probabilistic in nature, given the complex, multi-variant empirical environment in which they operate in constant interaction with semantic and pragmatic co-variants. The generalizations which result from this study will likewise be tendencies and context-sensitive, applicable in the majority of cases but not without exceptions.

1.3.4.3 Data and analysis

Taking the view that a proposed universal is best attested in languages that are genetically, geographically and typologically unrelated, this book investigates languages which are quite diverse genetically, geographically and typologically. Those examined range from Indo-European languages (e. g. English, Dutch, Breton, etc.), Sino-Tibetan languages (e. g. Chinese, etc.), Malayo-Polynesian languages (e. g. Samoan, Maori, Ivatan, Indonesian, etc.), Mayan languages (e. g. Quiche, Aguacatec, etc.), to African languages (Margi, Kinyarwanda, Kpelle, Tera, etc.), and other languages such as Hebrew and Basque. Altogether, a total of about 50 languages are studied to various extent in terms of clefting and cleftability.

There are two kinds of data sources used in this book. First, there is first-hand data collected in newspapers or daily conversations, such as some of the examples of Chinese and English. Other examples in this group are elicited from native speakers of Chinese or English on different occasions. The second kind of source, as a means of independent verification, includes most of the examples collected from publications which are (i) reference grammar books of different languages; (ii) journal articles on clefts and related topics, most of which deal with clefting but not cleftability. Where necessary and possible, consultations have been made for data confirmation.

Data analysis combines qualitative with quantitative analyses, and is descriptive in nature. While most analyses will largely be qualitative, based on the set of criteria set forth in 2. 1 and the principles proposed to account for cleftability, quantitative analysis is also carried out where necessary, especially in relation to frequency of occurrence of various kinds of cleft sentences both intralinguistically and crosslinguistically. The purpose of such a combination is to see whether the results of the qualitative analysis correspond to those of the quantitative analysis, with the belief that where they do match, evidence will be strongest either for or against the hypothesized Hierarchy.

Chapter 2 NP Cleftability

In this chapter, a set of criteria will be proposed for measuring cleftability of different positions on the Cleftability Hierarchy, followed by application of these criteria in analysis of crosslinguistic data of various kinds to see whether they support or reject the proposed Cleftability Hierarchy. In the next chapter, a detailed analysis of some apparent counterexamples will be presented to show how the Cleftability Hierarchy can interact with typological parameters and language-specific structural constraints.

2.1 The Cleftability Criteria

A set of criteria is set forth in (17) to determine relative cleftability of different syntactic positions on the Cleftability Hierarchy:

(17) A syntactic position X is more cleftable than another syntactic position Y if

a. X, but not Y, is cleftable;

b. X uses the deletion strategy more than Y and/or uses the pronoun retention strategy less than Y;

c. X can be clefted in a larger variety of sentences, or in more complex constructions, than Y;

d. X is clefted more frequently than Y, intralinguistically or crosslinguistically, in the same kind of texts;

e. promotion of a form from Y to X, but not vice versa, facilitates clefting of that form;

f. diachronic "cleftization" affects X before it does Y, resulting in a continuous segment of cleftable positions on the CH.

(17a) deals basically with grammaticality. Since the subject end of the Cleftability Hierarchy expresses the easiest or most natural positions to cleft, a simple case would be a language which can cleft only subjects but not any other positions, in which case subjects would be considered more cleftable than direct objects, indirect objects, etc. In other cases where several positions are cleftable, X and Y may stand for any segment involved in the comparison.

(17b) deals with clefting strategies used with different positions which are viewed as reflecting different degrees of cleftability. *Access* here refers to the applicability of a strategy with respect to the clefting of a certain position on the Cleftability Hierarchy. As discussed in 1.3.3, use of the pronoun retention strategy supposedly facilitates processing of those sentences in which a position low on the CH is clefted; while the deletion strategy, which results in a less transparent structure, is usually used with clefting of higher position(s) on the CH. According to our theory, this is made possible at least partly by the ease with which these higher positions are processed. As will be seen, sometimes, a language can use one of the strategies to cleft two or more positions, and the other to cleft only one of them. Therefore, a mere mention of either one of the strategies as measurement of cleftability would not always adequately reveal the difference in cleftability involved through the utilization of these strategies. As a hypothetical example, if a language can cleft subjects and direct objects using the pronoun retention strategy but can cleft only subjects using the deletion strategy, according to (17b), subjects will be considered more cleftable than direct objects. On the other hand, if we use only the pronoun retention strategy as a criterion, no such difference will be revealed, since both subjects and direct objects are susceptible to it. Therefore, (17b) mentions both strategies and the interactions thereof.

(17c) aims to measure degrees of cleftability in cases where two or more positions can be clefted with the same strategy. The assumption taken here is that difference in cleftability between different positions may be more likely revealed in semantically and structurally more complex sentences than in less complex ones. Thus, for example, difference in cleftability between direct objects and indirect objects which will not show up in affirmative sentences will probably show up in the corresponding negative sentences or embedded constructions. As another example, in languages which have a word order norm but which admit of variations on it with only very minor differences in meaning, we would expect, according to the theory, that word order freedom would decrease as we cleft NPs on the lower end of the CH, i.e. the more difficult the position clefted, the greater the tendency to choose the most unmarked order (Givón 1973, as cited in Keenan 1987, in *Supplement to CLS*).

(17d) uses frequency of occurrence to measure cleftability of different syntactic positions. Given that more frequent elements will be less marked (Givón 1990), and that more cleftable constituents will be less marked, the relationship between cleftability and frequency of occurrence can be expressed as "More cleftable constituents will occur more frequently."

It will be hypothesized that the frequency with which a constituent is clefted in discourse, both within a language and crosslinguistically, conforms to the Cleftability Hierarchy, i. e. subjects being the most frequent, then direct objects, indirect objects, etc.

(17e) presents a kind of "cooperation" between cleftability and promotion. Promotion is a common linguistic process whereby a given grammatical function (e. g. object or oblique NP) is either subjectivized or objectivized through syntactic means (e. g. passivization in English and other Indo-European languages) or morphological devices (e. g. detransitivization in Austronesian languages and Bantu languages (Givón 1979; Croft 1990). What (17e) says, then, is that since promotion facilitates clefting and other syntactic processes such as relativization (*ibid.*), if an uncleftable form which occurs as one grammatical function becomes cleftable after it is promoted to another grammatical function, then the function to which the form is promoted will be considered more cleftable. Presumably, the direction of promotion (e. g. from an oblique NP to direct object) will correspond to the right-to-left order on the CH.

Finally, (17f) predicts that if a previously uncleftable position becomes cleftable as a result of language change (called diachronic cleftization here), it must be the leftmost one of a segment of uncleftable positions on the Hierarchy. The consequence of such a change is a continuous segment of cleftable positions on the Hierarchy. The opposite case, in which cleftization of a position results in a discontinuous segment of cleftable positions on the Hierarchy, is highly unlikely. As a hypothetical example, consider (18), where the asterisks indicate uncleftable positions.

(18)	Stage 1:	a.	SU	*DO	*IO
	Stage 2:	b.	SU	DO	*IO
		*c.	SU	*DO	IO

As (18a) shows, a language may cleft only subjects at Stage 1. At Stage 2, one of the previously uncleftable positions becomes cleftable. Two possibilities exist for such cleftization: either the DO, or the IO, becomes cleftable, resulting in cleftability patterns shown in (18b) and (18c), respectively. Since (18b) represents a continuous, whereas (18c) a discontinuous, segment of cleftable positions on the CH, the former is a more plausible and more likely development in line with the Continuity Constraint, (2) and (15), discussed in Chapter 1. In terms of cleftability, if (18b) is attested but not (18c), then direct objects should be considered more cleftable than indirect objects.

It should be noted that while each of the above criteria may measure cleftability independently, they also act together as a clustering of features in the sense that the supporting evidence will be strongest where the greatest number of the criteria are met. Thus, according to the proposed Cleftability Hierarchy, subjects will exhibit the greatest number of the criterial features of higher cleftability, and those low on the CH will show the least features.

Finally, (17) will also serve as an organizational clue for this chapter. In the remaining part of the chapter, we will examine crosslinguistic data according to the order of the criteria: grammaticality, strategies, structural distribution/ complexity, frequency, promotion, and diachronic cleftization, to see if empirical evidence supports the proposed Cleftability Hierarchy.

2.2 Grammaticality: Cleftable Versus Uncleftable

2.2.1 Clefting of subject only

Since subject is supposed to be the easiest position to cleft, the Cleftability Hierarchy predicts that if a language can cleft any position at all, it should be able to cleft subject. The simplest case in support of the Cleftability Hierarchy, then, would be languages in which only subjects are cleftable. We will examine some languages of this kind below.

2.2.1.1 Chadic languages

2.2.1.1.1 Margi

Margi, a Chadic language spoken in Africa with a basic SVO word order, offers such an example. In Margi, the newly developed quasi-copula, *ŋu*, in nominal sentences can be used as a CFM marker, "introduced between subject and predicate, in order to give the subject a certain emphasis." (Hoffmann 1963:89). Although no apparent structural dislocation is involved, a cleft reading is actually in order:

(19) a. ni atsianyi (Hoffmann 1963)
I kill-3s
"I killed him."

b. *ni -ŋ* atsianyi
I CFM kill-him
"I killed him / it is I who killed him."

As can be seen, the only difference between (19a) and (19b) is the presence of the CFM *ŋu*, with appropriate stress on the focused constituent. As Hoffmann points out, only subjects can be thus used in Margi, which is predicted by (17a).

2.2.1.1.2 Bade, Ngizim, Karekare, and Dera

Whereas Margi, which belongs to the Biu-Mandara branch of the Chadic language family, presents cleft sentences with no apparent dislocation, some languages from the Plateau-Sahel branch of the same family have subject clefting with a different structure. Four such languages are discussed in Schuh (1971): Bade, Ngizim, Karekare, and Dera, which are sister languages and show an unmarked SVO word order. In these languages, again, only subjects can be clefted, and clefted subjects all occur post-verbally, differing only in details with regard to their exact positions and the use of clefting strategies. In other words, clefting in these languages is through right-dislocation.

Following are subject-clefting examples from Bade, Ngizim, Karekare and Dera, respectively. Since third person singular subjects take zero realization in verb agreement, only examples with non-third singular subjects are given for more explicit illustration.

Bade (Schuh 1971:69)

(20) a. nə zədə səraw
1s dug well
"I dug the well."

b. (nə) zədə səraw *ayu*
1s dug well I
"It is I who dug the well / *I* dug the well."

c. (nə) zədə-*k* *ayu* səraw
1s dug CFM I well
"It is I who dug the well / *I* dug the well."

Ngizim (Schuh 1971:71)

(21) a. ka dlamə papiya
2s do lie
"You lied."

b. ka dlamə papiya-*n* ci
2s do lie CFM you
"It's you who lied / *You* lied."

c. * dlamə papiya-*n ci*

Karekare (Schuh 1971:73)

(22) a. ku taadan agoogoo
2s break watch
"You broke the watch."

b. (ku) taadan agoogoo *na* *dəku*
2s break watch CFM you
"It's you who broke the watch / *You* broke the watch."

Dera (Schuh 1971:74)

(23) a. mə gopo-mu Sani
1P pass = by-1P Shani
"We passed by Shani."

b. gopo-mu Sani *məni*
pass = by-1P Shani we
"It is we who passed by Shani / *We* passed by Shani."

c. * mə gopo-mu Sani *məni*

First, let's look at the Bade data. (20a) is an unmarked sentence, which requires a verb agreement marker, in this case the subject pronoun clitic *nə*, which agrees in person, number and gender with the unsurfaced pronoun subject. In (20b), the subject is clefted by virtue of being right-dislocated to the end of the sentence, appearing as an independent subject pronoun. The appearance of the subject pronoun clitic *nə*, which functions as a pronominal copy of the clefted subject, is optional (Schuh 1971:70), which is represented in (20a) by appearing in brackets. In (20c), a variant of (20b), the subject is also right-dislocated, but to a post-verbal position before the direct object, and the preverbal pronoun clitic occurs optionally. The appearance of *-k* suffixed to the verb is interesting. Schuh (1971:70) points out that this *-k* is a marker inserted before a postposed subject, but only when it is adjacent to the verb. It is also argued here that the function of *-k* in Bade is, among other things, to disambiguate in the following sense. If we cleft a sentence equivalent to *The dog chased the cat* the way that (20c) is clefted, we will not be able to tell from the surface structure whether it means *It's the dog that chase the cat or It's the cat that chased the dog* without the presence of *-k*, since it is possible to postpose the subject either to the end position or to the position before the object. This is the case especially when the subject pronoun clitic is not used. However, if we use the verb suffix *-k*, no such ambiguity arises, because *-k* clearly indicates that what immediately follows it is a clefted subject, which is the only cleftable position in Bade.

It will further be argued that *-k* and the like are more closely associated with the clefted subject NP than with the verb, functioning as a CFM. There are two pieces of evidence for this argument crosslinguistically. First, as shown in Ngizim, (21b), and Karekare, (22b), in which clefted subjects occur only in final position and no ambiguity of the kind in Bade exists, an equivalent marker is present. Therefore, the marker can not be said to function as a disambiguator in these languages; the only possible function for it is to mark the focus. Secondly, we note that while the marker occurs morphologically as a verb suffix in Bade and Ngizim, its equivalent (very probably a cognate) occurs in Karekare as an independent word between the object and the clefted subject, as in (22b). Therefore, the marker does not always appear as a verbal suffix in related sister languages and cannot always be said to be more closely related to the verb than to the focused NP even morphologically. On the other hand, it is observed crosslinguistically that wherever the marker occurs, it is *always* adjacent to the clefted subject, a fact predicted by the functional principle that semantico-functionally related forms tend to be close to each other in the speech chain (Bybee 1985). Therefore, based on the above evidence, we can conclude that the marker *-k* in Bade functions as a CFM pragmatically, marking the focus of a cleft sentence, although morphologically it is a verbal suffix.

To sum up, only subjects can be clefted in Bade, and clefted subjects can occur either immediately after the verb before a direct object if any, or sentence-finally after the object, the latter being the unmarked pattern. The clefting strategy can be either deletion or pronoun retention.

Unlike Bade, Ngizim, Karekare and Dera all right-dislocate the clefted subject to the final position only; no pre-object dislocation is allowed. In terms of the clefting strategy, Ngizim can be said to allow retention but not deletion, as shown in a comparison between (21b) and (21c), where lack of a pronoun clitic, *ka*, for the clefted subject in (21c) renders the sentence ungrammatical. Karekare allows either deletion or retention, as shown by the optional subject pronoun clitic, *ku*, in (22b). Finally, Dera allows only deletion, as shown by the grammaticality of (23b), where no pronoun clitic is used in the cleft construction, and the ungrammaticality of (23c), where a subject pronoun clitic is used.

For synthesis of information on crosslinguistic patterns of cleftability later in this chapter, the subject-clefting patterns for the four Chadic languages discussed in this section are summarized as in Table 2.1:

Table 2.1 ***The subject-clefting patterns in Bade, Ngizim, Karekare, and Dera***

	Bade	Ngizim	Karekare	Dera
Deletion	+	−	+	+
Retention	+	+	+	−

2.2.1.2 Toba-Batak

In Toba-Batak, a VSO language, the subject can be preposed through topicalization, and once topicalized can be further marked for emphasis with a focus marker, *do*, which immediately follows the subject (Percival 1981:114).

(24) a. mangoli au
come-buy-wife I
"I come to buy a wife."

b. *au do* na mangoli (Von der Tuuk 1971:343)
I CFM COMP come-buy-wife
"It is I who come to buy a wife."

In (24), the topicalized subject, *au*, is followed by *do*, the focus marker, which serves to contrastively focus the constituent which precedes it. It is noted that only subject can be thus focused, and such subject-focusing is found only in topicalized sentences but "not in other types of sentences". (Percival 1981:114)

2.2.1.3 Indonesian

In formal Indonesian, an SVO language, as depicted in most Indonesian grammars, clefting, which puts the focused constituent sentence-initially and separates it from the rest of the sentence by the complementizer *yang*, is restricted to subjects only. The focused NP is left-dislocated without leaving behind a resumptive pronoun, i. e. via the deletion strategy, and no CFM is present, as in (25):

(25) a. dokter itu me-meriksa saya (Chung 1978)
doctor the TRANS-examine 1s
"The doctor examined me."

b. *dokter itu yang* me-meriksa saya
doctor the COMP TRANS-examine 1s
"It was the doctor that examined me."

Direct objects and other syntactic positions on the Cleftability Hierarchy as a rule cannot be thus clefted (Chung 1978). For example, in (26),

(26) * *saya yang* dokter itu me-meriksa
1s COMP doctor the TRANS-examine
"It was me that the doctor examined."

the direct object *saya* "I/me" occurs sentence-initially as the cleft focus, to render the sentence ungrammatical.

2.2.1.4 Malagasy

A slightly more complicated situation is found in Malagasy, in which clefting shows some interesting difference from relativization. As a VOS language (Harries-Delisle 1978: 431), Malagasy has cleft focus in the initial position, immediately followed by the focus marker *no*; and no resumptive pronoun is used in the presupposed part. In Keenan (1977), Malagasy is listed as one of the languages which can only have their subjects relativized. One would expect this to be true of clefting in Malagasy; however, the following sentences show that adjuncts (of time) in (28) as well as subjects in (27b) can be clefted in Malagasy:

(27) a. niteny ny lehilahy (Keenan 1985: 170)
spoke the man
"The man spoke."

b. *ny lehilahy no* niteny
the man CFM spoke
"It was the man who spoke."

(28) *ela no* tsy nahitako anao (Harries-Delisle 1978: 428)
long-time CFM not see-1s 2s
"It's a long time that I didn't see you."

The facts shown here are not necessarily in conflict with what Keenan claims with respect to relativization. This is because clefting and relativization, with all their similarities, are two different syntactic processes, each operating within its own domain. More specifically, the operational domain for clefting in general includes non-NPs as well as NPs, whereas that for relativization is limited to NPs only. Such difference in operational domains in part accounts for cleftability of NP adjuncts (of time) in Malagasy, which in general behave like PPs by virtue of their adverbiality. Such adverbials, in particular those of location and time, tend to enjoy high cleftability. In fact, as will be shown in Chapter 4, in many languages, such adverbials have nearly as high cleftability as subjects. Therefore, given the domain factor, if we temporarily set aside non-NP clefting and look only at NP clefting, Malagasy may still be said to be a language which can cleft only subjects in terms of NP clefting.

2.2.2 Clefting of NP arguments

Many languages can cleft other NP arguments as well as subjects. When they do so, the Continuity Constraint (15) predicts that the cleftable constituents form a continuous segment on the Cleftability Hierarchy, without leaving a gap. This is attested in many languages, of which Basque and Berber are two examples.

2.2.2.1 Basque

Basque is a language spoken in the area between France and Spain, a genetically isolated language possibly affiliated with Caucasian languages. It is a morphologically ergative language, but appears syntactically accusative (Saltarelli et al. 1988). Although Basque has rather free word order, its neutral order seems to be SOV. Roughly, the cleft sentence in Basque takes the form

F_i copula/CFM [s. . . $\underline{e_i}$. . . Comp]

where F is the focused constituent, CFM function is assumed by the copula, S is something like a headless relative clause with a missing constituent coindexed with F, and Comp is the complementizer. The preverbal focus position can be occupied by an NP, which corresponds to a missing coindexed NP within S. In other words, deletion is the sole strategy used for clefting. In terms of cleftability, both subject and object are cleftable in this way. To wit,

(29) a. *ama* *izan* d-a soineko-a jos-i d-u-en-a
mother(sA) was 3A-PRES dress-sA sewed 3A-AUX-COMP-sA
"It was mother who sewed the dress." (Saltarelli et al. 1988)

b. *soineko-a izan* d-a ama-k jos-i d-u-en-a
dress(A) was 3A-PRES mother-sE sewed 3A-AUX-COMP-sA
"It was the dress that mother sewed."

In (29a), what is clefted is the subject, which is not recapitulated by any resumptive pronoun in the presupposed clause except an agreement pronominal suffix on the auxiliary verb, which also shows up in the corresponding non-cleft sentence. In (29b), the clefted constituent is the direct object, which, like subject clefting, shows up initially and does not leave behind any resumptive pronoun. The bi-clausal nature of the cleft construction is seen in the clefted subject in (29a), whose marking changes from ergative to absolutive, because it is now structurally governed by the copula/CFM and separated from the presupposed clause by an S-boundary.

With indirect object, however, clefting is questionable:

(30) ? *Miren* *d- a* Jon-ek liburu-a ema-n z-io-n-a
Mary(A) 3A-PRES-(be) John-E book-sA gave 3sE-3sD-COMP-sA
"It is Mary that John gave the book to."

The dative case in the questionable (30) is reflected in the dative (D) agreement prefix *io-* on the Comp toward the end of the sentence. Since no postposition is present, the problem of (30) can not be imputed to a stranded postposition, as in some other languages. The dubious grammaticality of indirect object clefting, then, shows that indirect objects are less cleftable than subjects or direct objects in Basque.

Finally, clefting of oblique NPs is simply ruled out:

(31) * *ama(-ri)* *d-a* (za-io) liburu-a eros-i d-io-da-n-a
mother(-for) 3A-PRES = be AUX-3sB book-sA buy-PERF sA-3sB-1sE-COMP-sA
"It is mother/for mother that I've bought the book (for)."

Oblique NPs with different semantic roles such as benefactive are all ruled out as uncleftable. It should be noted that, unlike in some other languages, the benefactive case in Basque does not merge with the dative case, and shows its independence by being treated differently with respect to clefting.

(32)	S	DO	IO	OBL
Clefting	+	+	?	–

(32) summarizes cleftability of NP arguments in Basque, which conforms to the suggested Cleftability Hierarchy in two senses. First, the ordering of constituents from the most to the least cleftable follows the ordering on the Hierarchy. For example, indirect objects are shown to be less cleftable than either subjects or direct objects but

more cleftable than oblique NPs. Secondly, for the fully grammatical sentences, the clefting strategy applies to a continuous segment on the Hierarchy, in this case subject and direct object, which are adjacent to each other. (32), then, can be represented as (33), where the equation mark = indicates that there is no attested difference in cleftability between subject and direct object. (33) conforms to the Cleftability Hierarchy, (3).

(33) SU = DO > IO > OBL

2.2.2.2 Berber

Berber has a basic word order of VSO, although SVO, OVS, SOV and OSV are all attested. The cleft construction is exemplified below:

(34) a. i-umz hmad iqaridn (Ennaji & Sadiqi 1986)
he-received Ahmed money
"Ahmed received the money."

b. *hmad* a i-umz-n iqaridn
Ahmed COMP 3s-received-INF money
"It's Ahmed who received the money."

c. *iqaridn* a i-umz hmad
money COMP 3s-received Ahmed
"It's the money that Ahmed received."

(34b-c) differ from (34a) in that the focused constituents occur in sentence-initial position, and that the Complementizer *a* appears immediately after the focus. Therefore, clefting in Berber left-dislocates the cleft focus to a preverbal position, followed by a clause boundary marking Comp *a*. In (34b), the form *-n* is a non-finite participial form which "shows tense but not person or number distinctions" (Ennaji & Sadiqi 1986:56).

Apart from subject and direct object, other constituents are also cleftable in Berber, such as indirect objects (35), oblique NPs (36), PP adverbials (37), and temporal NPs (38) (Ennaji & Sadiqi 1986: 56, 69).

(35) *argaz* a mi i-fa hmad iqaridn
man COMP to 3s-gave Ahmed money
"It's the man that Ahmed gave the money to."

(36) *lqum* a f ksud-R
children COMP about worried-I
"It's the children who I am worried about."

(37) a. *ddaw ttabla* a g t-zra lktab
under table COMP at she-saw book
"It was under the table that she saw the book."
b. *f lkursi* a f i-qqim augaz
on chair COMP on 3s-sat man
"It was on the chair that the man sat."

(38) *assant* a i-dda hmad
yesterday COMP 3s-went Ahmed
"It was yesterday that Ahmed left."

(39) *abxxan* a i-ga hmad
black COMP 3s-is Ahmed
"* It's black that Ahmed is."

In terms of the clefting strategy, it is clear that subject and direct object clefting uses deletion, as in (34b) and (34c), respectively. For indirect object clefting, the *mi* in (35) is different in form from the dative marker *i* which occurs in the corresponding non-cleft sentence. According to Ennaji & Sadiqi (1986:57), *mi*, being a kind of complex morpheme, is a variant of *i* and is in complementary distribution with *i*. Therefore, it can be said that *mi* is a kind of stranded preposition, and that indirect object clefting also employs the deletion strategy. This is supported by (36), where an oblique NP is clefted, since the *f* "about" in (36), being a simple morpheme, is clearly a stranded preposition.

However, the picture is complicated by (37), where the whole PP is clefted but there is still a stranded preposition, *g* "at" or *f* "about", in the position from which the PP has been dislocated. The simple phonological shape of the stranded preposition renders highly unlikely the prospect to analyze it as morphologically complex. Functionally, however, we may say that while prepositions in Berber can stand stranded, as in (35-36), they may also function as resumptive pro-PPs, as in (37). Otherwise, it will be difficult to account for the occurrence thereof in sentences like (37). Therefore, in (37), the single preposition acts as a pro-form for the whole PP that has been dislocated, a case of the retention strategy, except that what is being retained is not a pronoun but a pro-PP. The same use, however, does not apply to sentences like (35) and (36), simply because what is clefted is not a PP but a presumably more cleftable NP.

As for genitive NPs, they can not be clefted irrespective of the strategy used (Ennaji & Sadiqi 1986:62):

(40) a. t-zra ttomobil n hmad
she-saw car of Ahmed
"She saw Ahmed's car."

b. * *hmad* a t-zra ttomobil n
Ahmed COMP she-saw car of
"* It's Ahmed that she saw the car of."

To sum up, the cleftability pattern in Berber is given as in Table 2.2:

Table 2.2 ***The cleftability pattern in Berber***

<table>
<tr><th></th><th>SU</th><th>DO</th><th>IO</th><th>OBL</th><th>GEN</th><th>PP</th><th>ADVL/Temp NP</th></tr>
<tr><td>Deletion</td><td>+</td><td>+</td><td>+</td><td>+</td><td>−</td><td></td><td rowspan="2">+</td></tr>
<tr><td>Retention</td><td></td><td></td><td></td><td></td><td>−</td><td>+</td></tr>
</table>

Note that all NP constituents are clefted with the deletion strategy. In terms of (17a), we can represent the cleftability of different NP constituents in Berber as in (41), while postponing the discussion on PP- and ADVL-clefting to Chapter 4. Again, (41) supports the proposed Cleftability Hierarchy in the sense that there is no counterevidence against the CH, and that all the cleftable positions form a continuous segment on the CH:

(41) SU = DO = IO = OBL > GEN

2.3 Clefting Strategies: Deletion Versus Retention

2.3.1 Polynesian languages

Most if not all of the Polynesian languages have VSO(X) as their basic word order. These languages often show syntactic properties that lend evidence in various ways to support the proposed Cleftability Hierarchy in terms of (17b). Among the languages examined are Maori, Tongan, Somoan, Rennellese, and Pukapukan, in which a focused NP can be clefted through left dislocation, usually with the focused constituent marked by a sentence-initial predicate particle which functions as a CFM.

Transitive verbs in many Polynesian languages can further be classified into canonical transitive and middle transitive, based largely on their semantics.

Canonical transitive verbs describe events which produce a direct, often physical effect on the direct object, while middle verbs describe events that do not affect the direct object immediately. Common types of middle verbs include perception verbs, verbs of emotion and other psychological states (e. g. *love*, *want*, and *understand*), and verbs normally selecting animate direct objects (*meet with*, *help*, *call*, *follow*, *wait for*, and *visit*). Chung (1978) calls transitive clauses with middle verbs "middle clauses". Middle clause direct objects are less DO-like in that the clauses exhibit a separate case pattern which resembles that used for intransitive clauses with an oblique NP (Chung 1978). According to the Cleftability Hierarchy, we will assume that middle clause direct objects are less cleftable than canonical clause direct objects.

2.3.1.1 Maori

There are two strategies used for clefting in Maori: deletion and pronoun retention. As mentioned earlier, deletion simply leaves a gap where the focused NP has been dislocated, and pronoun retention leaves behind a pronominal (clitic) copy of the dislocated NP. If we take the position that "the preservation of superficial sentential form [via pronoun retention] allows a rule access to structures which would otherwise be less accessible" (Cole *et al.* 1977: 40), and that pronoun retention strategy is "only minimally disruptive in terms of case recoverability" (Givón 1990:655), then pronoun retention is seen to increase the accessibility of certain kinds of clefted NPs that would have been uncleftable or less cleftable. According to Criterion (17b), given two NPs which have different grammatical roles, the one that can be clefted via deletion is considered to be more accessible than the one that can be clefted via pronoun retention. More generally, in terms of the interaction of the two strategies, the NP that enjoys more freedom in using the deletion strategy and/or less freedom in using the retention strategy is judged to be more accessible to clefting. Thus, in the case where the subject can be clefted via deletion but not retention whereas the direct object can be clefted via either deletion or retention, the subject would be considered more accessible than the direct object. As mentioned in 1.3.3, a plausible account for this is that the resumptive pronoun helps keep the underlying structure more transparent and therefore facilitates processing.

In Maori, both subject and direct object can be clefted through left dislocation, with the cleft focus marked by the CFM *ko*. In terms of the clefting strategy, subject is clefted through deletion, as in (42a), whereas a clefted direct object leaves behind a pronominal copy, *ai*, as in (42b) (Chung 1978):

(42) a. *ko Hone* tonu e horo nei i nga ika o to waka
CFM John still NONPST swallow this ACC the-PL fish of your canoe
"It is John who is swallowing the fish in your canoe!" (p. 69)

b. *ko te poaka* i hiahia *ai* a Hone ki te patu
CFM the pig PST want 3s PROP John COMP kill
"It is the pig that John wanted to kill."

In (42a), the cleft focus *Hone* "John" would be the subject in a corresponding non-cleft sentence, and the resumptive pronoun, *ai*, which is present in (42b), is not used in (42a). The difference between the two sentences is basically one of clefting strategy: deletion for subject clefting and pronoun retention for direct object clefting. Since the pronoun retention strategy is supposedly more marked than the deletion strategy according to (17b), direct objects have been shown to be less accessible to clefting than subjects in Maori.

2.3.1.2 Tongan

In Tongan, the clefting strategy used depends on the grammatical function of a focused NP. In general, the deletion strategy is used in sentences with clefted subjects. Interestingly, subject clefting shows a somewhat splitting pattern, in that with third person singular subjects of intransitive clauses, only deletion can be used in clefting; on the other hand, third person singular subjects of transitive clauses can be clefted using either deletion or pronoun retention (Chung 1978: 227-8):

(43) a. *ko e tamasi'i* 'oku (* **ne**) va'inga 'i mui
CFM the child PROG 3s play in back
"It is the child that is playing in the back."

b. *ko hoku tokoua* ' oku (**ne**) haka 'a e ika
CFM my sibling PROG 3s cook ABS the fish
"It is my brother who is cooking the fish."

The cleft focus in (43a) is the (third person singular) subject (*e tamasi'i*) of an intransitive clause with the intransitive verb *va'inga* "play"; therefore, only deletion is allowed. (43b), where the cleft focus is the (third person singular) subject (*hoku tokoua*) of a transitive clause with the transitive verb *haka* "cook", allows either deletion or pronoun retention by virtue of using the pronoun *ne*. A possible explanation of this discrepancy in terms of obligatoriness of the deletion strategy in intransitive and transitive sentences is that in ergative languages like Tongan, intransitive subjects are more "subject-like" than transitive subjects, in that they are *always* treated as subjects whether syntactically paired with transitive subjects (i. e. the accusative pattern) or with direct objects (i. e. the ergative pattern). On the other hand, a transitive subject may be treated like a non-subject if the language exhibits syntactic ergativity in one way or another. The greater possibility for transitive subjects to exhibit non-subject behaviour, it is reasoned, accounts at least in part for their greater flexibility with regard to the choice of the clefting strategy in question. We will return to a more detailed discussion about clefting in ergative languages in 3. 1.

A similar split in subject clefting occurs in middle clauses where the clefted subject behaves like a third person singular transitive subject, in that it allows either the deletion or the pronoun retention strategy:

(44) *ko* *Mele* 'oku (**ne**) fakamalo ki he tangata (Chung 1978:229)
CFM Mary PROG 3s thank to the man
"It is Mary who was thanking the man."

By definition, the verb *fakamalo* "thank" in (44) is a middle verb. When the subject *Mele* "Mary" is clefted, the resumptive pronoun *ne* may appear in the subject position in the presupposed clause (i. e. pronoun retention), although its occurrence is not obligatory.

As for direct objects and oblique NPs, the deletion strategy is required for the former, and the pronoun retention strategy, for the latter:

(45) *ko* *hai* 'oku ke fiema'u (* **ai**) ke ne 'ave mama'o ho'o tivi?
CFM who PROG you want 3s SBJN 3s take far your T. V.
"Who is it that you want to take your T. V. away?" (Chung 1978:230-1)

(46) a. *ko* *hai* 'oku mahino ki * (**ai**) 'a e lea faka-Tonga?
CFM who PROG clear to 3s ABS the language Tongan
"Who understands the Tongan language (lit. whom is the Tongan language clear to)?"

b. *ko* *e* *lao* kuo pau ke talangofua kotoa ki * (**ai**)
CFM the law PERF must SBJN obey all to PRO
"It is the law that everyone must obey."

In (45), what is clefted is an underlying direct object of the verb *fiema'u* "want". Accordingly, the deletion strategy is used and the presence of a pronominal copy *ai* is disallowed, as indicated by the asterisk inside the brackets. In (46a-b), where an oblique NP to the preposition *ki* is clefted, the opposite is true: the presence of *ai* is obligatory and its deletion is not possible, as indicated by the asterisk outside the brackets.

Direct objects of middle clauses are treated like oblique NPs when clefted or relativized, by virtue of the required pronoun retention strategy:

(47) a. *ko* *hoku tuofefine* 'oku nau manako ai
CFM my sister PROG they like PRO
"It is my sister that they like."

b. * *ko hoku tuofefine* 'oku nau manako
CFM my sister PROG they like

(47) uses middle verbs which are less transitive than canonical transitive verbs. Unlike in English, direct objects of these middle verbs pattern after oblique objects in clefts or relative clauses in that they must overtly express the dependency relationship between the cleft focus / head noun and the gap in the clause by virtue of a resumptive pronoun.

Therefore, in terms of clefting (and relativization), subjects of middle clauses in Tongan are treated like third person singular transitive subjects, and direct objects of middle clauses are treated like oblique NPs, a degradation of cleftability by one degree, so to speak, in both cases. As will be seen shortly, this same pattern exists in other Polynesian languages as well. The issue here is presumably one of interaction between cleftability and transitivity, to which we will return shortly in 2.3.1.3.

Table 2.3 sums up the uses of clefting strategies in Tongan:

Table 2.3 ***The clefting strategies in relation to cleftable constituents in Tongan***

	SU_{vi}	DO	SU_{vt3s}	SU_m	OBL	DO_m
Deletion	+	+	+	+	–	–
Retention	–	–	+	+	+	+

The pluses and minuses in Table 2.3 represent an ordered scale of cleftability according to (17b): $SU_{vi} = DO > SU_{vi3s} = SU_m > OBL = DO_m$, which shows an apparent discord with the Cleftability Hierarchy. Although the strategies used or forbidden do form a continuous segment on the Cleftability Hierarchy, the split pattern for subjects results in a hierarchy which at least in part shows higher cleftability of direct objects over third person singular transitive subjects (SU_{vt3s}), something contrary to the SU > DO sequence of the Cleftability Hierarchy. However, as pointed out earlier, this patterning also reveals a kind of ergative pattern which is found in many languages including Tongan, i. e. S (ubject) and P (atient) are grouped together as against A (gent) with regard to the way in the use of clefting strategies. A more detailed account of the relationship between accusative and ergative languages in terms of grammatical roles and their interpretation in relation to the Cleftability Hierarchy will be given in 3. 1. For the moment, let's just assume that direct objects behave like intransitive subjects and transitive subjects behave like direct objects in syntactically ergative languages. Thus interpreted, the results shown in Table 2. 3 do not contradict the Cleftability Hierarchy.

2.3.1.3 Samoan

In another Polynesian language, Samoan, both subject clefting and direct object clefting use the deletion, but not the retention, strategy, the only difference being that while subject clefting requires the presence of a transitive suffix *-ina* which is attached to a transitive verb in a transitive clause, direct object clefting does not. This is exemplified in (48), where (48b) shows that retention is not allowed when clefting a direct object.

(48) a. *'o* *le* *'afa* sa fa'aleaga-ina fale
CFM the storm PST destroy-TRANS house
"It was the storm that destroyed the houses."

b. *'o* *tamaiti* *nei* na (ia) maua (* **latou**)
CFM children these PST he catch them
"It is these children that he found."

On the other hand, if an oblique NP is clefted, as in (49a), the retention strategy is in order, in exclusion of the deletion strategy, as shown in (49b). Thus the only difference between (49a) and (49b) is the presence versus absence of the pro-form *ai*.

(49) a. *'o* *le* *fale'oloa* sa ' ou maua **ai** Ioane 'o gaoi niu
CFM the store PST I catch PRO(3s) John COMP steal coconut
"It was in the store that I caught John stealing the coconuts."

b. * *'o* *le* *fale'oloa* sa 'ou maua Ioane 'o gaoi niu
CFM the store PST I catch JohnCOMP steal coconut

Just as in Tongan, direct objects of middle clauses in Samoan are treated like oblique NPs by virtue of being required to leave behind a pronominal copy after clefting:

(50) *'o* *ai* na ia agaleaga ki ai? (Chung 1978:236)
CFM who PST he mistreat to PRO(3s)
"Who is it that he mistreated?"

The pairing of middle clause direct objects with oblique NPs in Samoan is further evidenced by morphological marking. Middle clause direct objects are case marked with *ki* "to" or *'i* "at". Thus marked, they are treated like oblique NPs whose case marking they share. For example, when middle clause direct objects marked with *ki* or oblique NPs marked with *ki* are clefted, both are pronominalized to *ki ai*, as seen in (50); when middle clause direct objects marked with *'i* or oblique NPs marked with *'i* are clefted, both are pronominalized to *ai*.

A possible account of this phenomenon involves transitivity and subsequent case marking. Put it simply, middle verbs, e.g. verbs of perception and communication, are less transitive than canonical transitive verbs in that they affect the state of being of their objects to a lesser degree than canonical transitive verbs; therefore, they are conceptually more distant from the verb than objects of canonical transitive verbs. This lesser degree of transitivity and greater conceptual distance is coded morphologically by adding an extra case marker on the middle clause object NP, resulting in greater linguistic distance between it and the verb, an exemplification of an iconicity principle, *viz.* the Proximity Principle (Haiman 1985; Givón 1990; Croft 1990; Newmeyer 1992). Once thus marked, middle clause objects are treated in the same way as other oblique NPs in syntactic processes such as clefting and relativization. Therefore, cleftability in Tongan and Samoan relies not only on grammatical relations, but also on semantic notions like transitivity.

In sum, the use of clefting strategies in relation to cleftable constituents is shown in Table 2.4.

Table 2.4 ***The clefting strategies in relation to cleftable constituents in Samoan***

	SUB	DO	OBL*
Deletion	+	+	–
Retention	–	–	+

* OBL includes direct objects of middle clauses.

2.3.1.4 Rennellese

Rennellese belongs to the Samoic-Outlier subgroup of the Malayo-Polynesian language family. Clefting in Rennellese involves a sentence-initial focus NP which is marked by the CFM *ko*. In Rennellese, intransitive subjects and canonical transitive direct objects are clefted via the deletion strategy, whereas NPs with oblique case marking, e. g. *i* "at", via the pronoun retention strategy (Chung 1978:289ff). For example:

(51) a. *ko te tinana*$_i$ kua kai e te tamana $\underline{e}_i$ (Elbert & Monberg 1965:351)
CFM the mother PERF eat ERG the father
"It was the mother who the father had eaten."
b. *ko ba'i 'aso* e ta'anga hano **ai** au ki mouku
CFM each day PRS PRS go 3s I to bush
"Every day... I come up here to the bush."

in (51a), the clefted constituent is a canonical transitive direct object and the deletion strategy is used. The e_i indicates a dependency relationship between the position and the cleft focus. The cleft focus in (51b) is a temporal NP treated in Rennellese as an oblique NP, as can be seen from the presence of *ai*, an oblique marking resumptive pronoun.

Middle clause direct objects, which are marked with *i* "at", pattern after oblique NPs and are clefted through the pronoun retention strategy:

(52) *ko koe* a'u ai au, kau kakabe-'ia
CFM you reach PRO 1s I take-TRANS
"It is you that I've come for and will take away."

Table 2.5 summarizes the use of clefting strategies in relation to the syntactic positions concerned.

Table 2.5 ***Clefting strategies in relation to cleftable constituents in Rennellese***

	S_{vi}	DO	OBL	DO_m
Deletion	+	+		
Retention			+	+

2.3.2 Summary

Table 2.6 summarizes the use of clefting strategies, with regard to grammatical functions of the focused NP, in Maori, Tongan, Somoan and Rennellese. Similar patterns are also found in other Polynesian languages such as Pukapukan. For subject clefting, all the languages can use the deletion strategy, and it is doubted that pronoun retention can be used at all except with Tongan third person singular transitive subject, which, due to its ergative pattern, is to be discussed in 3. 1. For direct object clefting, restriction on using the retention strategy is relaxed, in that some languages (for example, Maori and Pukapukan) unmarkedly use the retention strategy. For oblique NPs, which subsume indirect objects, no language seems to allow for deletion: pronoun retention applies exclusively. Or, in a weaker statement, pronoun retention is greatly preferred to deletion for clefting of oblique NPs.

To conclude this section, we interpret and formalize Criterion (17b) as

(53) [+ del, − ret] > [+ del, + ret] > [− del, + ret]

with respect to clefted NPs of different kinds, where [± del] represents (non-) use of the deletion strategy and [± ret], (non-) use of the retention strategy. What Table 6 shows, then, lends support to the proposed Cleftability Hierarchy in the following way: SUB > DO > IO/OBL.

Table 2. 6 ***Use of clefting strategies in terms of grammatical function in some Polynesian languages***

<table>
<tr><th rowspan="2">Language</th><th rowspan="2">Strategy</th><th colspan="2">Subject</th><th rowspan="2">DO</th><th rowspan="2">IO/OBL</th></tr>
<tr><th>vi.</th><th>vt.</th></tr>
<tr><td>Maori</td><td>Deletion</td><td colspan="2">+</td><td></td><td></td></tr>
<tr><td></td><td>Retention</td><td colspan="2"></td><td>+</td><td></td></tr>
<tr><td>Tongan</td><td>Deletion</td><td>+</td><td>+</td><td>+</td><td>−</td></tr>
<tr><td></td><td>Retention</td><td>−</td><td>+</td><td>−</td><td>+</td></tr>
<tr><td>Samoan</td><td>Deletion</td><td colspan="2">+</td><td>+</td><td>−</td></tr>
<tr><td></td><td>Retention</td><td colspan="2">−</td><td>−</td><td>+</td></tr>
<tr><td>Rennellese</td><td>Deletion</td><td colspan="2">+</td><td>+</td><td></td></tr>
<tr><td></td><td>Retention</td><td colspan="2"></td><td></td><td>+</td></tr>
<tr><td>Pukapukan</td><td>Deletion</td><td colspan="2">+</td><td></td><td></td></tr>
<tr><td></td><td>Retention</td><td colspan="2"></td><td>+</td><td>+</td></tr>
</table>

Note: Unspecified areas indicate lack of information.

2.4 Structural Complexity: Wider Versus Narrower Distribution

Different degrees of cleftability between NPs of various grammatical functions are sometimes difficult to discern, especially when NP positions are adjacent on the Cleftability Hierarchy and appear equally cleftable with regard to certain clefting strategies. For example, in English, all the syntactic positions on the Cleftability Hierarchy can be clefted with the same deletion strategy and all seem to be equally cleftable as far as grammaticality is concerned. Very often there is no reliable elicited judgment of cleftability even on the part of native speakers. Methodologically, however, one helpful criterion in measuring cleftability in such cases is (17c), which states that a more accessible constituent tends to be cleftable in more kinds of sentences or in more complex constructions, i. e. in wider distribution. Thus, other things being equal, if a constituent X can be clefted in negative as well as positive sentences but another constituent Y can only be clefted in positive sentences, X would be regarded as more cleftable than Y according to (17c). Also, it is possible sometimes to compare accessibility of different constituents by clefting them in more complex constructions which are usually considered "unpenetratable" by certain syntactic operations. Moreover, in some cases, greater cleftability of a given constituent is accounted for by the combined forces of more than one factors given in (17). Evidence from several languages supports these claims.

2.4.1 Maori

In 2.3.1.1, subjects in Maori are shown to be more accessible to clefting than direct objects, by virtue of using the deletion strategy for subject clefting but the pronoun retention strategy for direct object clefting. It is found that the lower cleftability of direct objects relative to subjects is also manifested in the fact that in negative sentences, which presumably have semantically and syntactically more complex structures, while subjects can be clefted in its usual way, direct objects are not cleftable even if the pronoun retention strategy is used. Thus consider

(54) a. * *ko te poaka* kahore **ai** i patu a Hera (Chung 1978:140)
CFM the pig not PRO3s PST kill prop Sara
"It is the pig that Sara didn't kill."

b. * *ko te kumara* kahore **ai** a Hone i waru
CFM the sweet-potato not PRO3s prop John PST peel
"It is the sweet potato that John didn't peel."

c. * *ko* *te* *wahine* kinai **ai** i tuku te tangata
CFM the woman not PRO3s PST release the man
"It is the woman that the man didn't release."

In the ungrammatical (54a-c), the cleft foci are all direct objects, and in each case a resumptive pronoun clitic *ai* is used before the verb of the presupposed clause. That the ungrammaticality is due to clefting of a direct object in a negative clause is clearly seen in a comparison of (54a-c) with an earlier sentence (42b), repeated here as (55), in which a direct object clefted in an affirmative sentence using the pronoun retention strategy is fully grammatical.

(55) *ko* *te* *poaka* i hiahia **ai** a Hone ki te patu
CFM the pig PST want PRO3s Prop John COMP kill
"It is the pig that John wanted to kill."

Therefore, by both (17b) and (17c), the Maori data support the Cleftability Hierarchy.

2.4.2 English

As mentioned in the beginning of this section, English in general does not distinguish between different clefting strategies; thus cleftability between different constituents on the Cleftability Hierarchy seems hard to measure by (17a) or (17b). If, however, we can find some constructions where subject clefting does make a difference in degrees of grammaticality from, say, direct object clefting, then by (17c), we can say that subjects are more cleftable than direct objects in English. Such a construction does exist, as shown by (56) and (57):

(56) a. ?* It is to please John that is easy.
b. * It is to please John that she expects.

(57) a. ? It is that he was so apologetic that surprised me. (Huddleston 1988:186)
b. * It is that she would reconsider her decision that she said.

Both (56) and (57) involve clefting of sentential subjects. The sentential subjects are small clauses (i. e. infinitives) in (56), and finite clauses in (57). Structurally, such a sentential clause is presumably dominated by an NP node, which accounts for their subject NP status. Doubtlessly, such a construction is more complex than a simple NP. An informal questionnaire was used to attest relative grammaticality between (56a) and (56b), and the majority of the native speaker respondents judged (56a) as less problematic than (56b). This result is supported by similar grammaticality judgement of (57) from Huddleston (1988). Since the a-sentences in (56) and (57) involve subject clefting whereas the b-sentences involve direct object clefting, a difference in cleftability between subjects and direct objects in English is attested as SU > DO, as predicted by (17c), in support of the Cleftability Hierarchy.

2.4.3 Danish

Danish provides another interesting case of different cleftability between subjects and direct objects, which is revealed only in more complex constructions. In Danish, as in English, cleft sentences in general take the form

expletive *it* be F_i [$_{s'}$ COMP [... e_i...]]

and both subjects and objects can be thus clefted, as shown in (58a) and (58b), respectively:

(58) a. det var *mig* der k∅bte den jakke (Smits 1989: 266)
it was me COMP bought this coat
"It was I who bought this coat."
b. det var *den jakke* som Björn k∅bte
it was this coat COMP Björn bought
"It was this coat that Björn bought."

Although both subjects and direct objects in Danish are cleftable, their cleftability differs with respect to certain constructions in which the cleft focus is part of a larger NP in the underlying structure. One such construction involves clefting of a genitive NP, as shown in (59).

(59) a. det var *kaptajn S∅rensen* hvis matroser sang for droningen
it was Captain S∅rensen whosesailors sang for the = queen
"It was Captain S∅rensen whose sailors sang for the queen."
b. *? det er *borgmesteren*, hvis l∅n droningen fastsætter
it is the = mayor whose wages the = queen determine
"It is the mayors whose wages the queen determines."

In both (59a) and (59b), a genitive NP has been clefted, which involves its movement out of the NP in which it is embedded. Compared with (58), (59) involves movement of the focus NP from more deeply embedded positions and therefore the construction is considered more complex than in (58). It is also noted that while (59a), in which the cleft focus is part of the subject of the presupposed clause, is fully grammatical, (59b) is problematic, in which the cleft focus is part of the direct object of the presupposed clause. In other words, what determines cleftability in this more complex construction is whether the cleft focus is part of the subject or part of the direct object of the presupposed clause. Since the former facilitates, whereas the latter prohibits, clefting of a genitive NP in this situation, subjects are more accessible to clefting than direct objects in Danish.

2.4.4 Kinyarwanda

In Kinyarwanda, a Bantu language with a basic SVO order, there are two kinds of cleft constructions in addition to a pseudo-cleft construction, both using a CFM *ni*, which is identical in form with the copula.

The first cleft pattern, Cleft 1, is used in response to *who/what* questions (Kimenyi 1978). Its structural configuration can be formulated as (60):

(60) CFM F_i [$_{S'}$ REL [$_S$... e_i...]]

where the focused constituent is left-dislocated without leaving behind a resumptive pronoun. Cleft 1 is applicable to subjects, direct objects, indirect objects and oblique NPs, but not to genitive NPs. (61b-d) are examples of subject, direct object and indirect object clefting, respectively.

(61) a. umukoòbwa y-a-haa-ye úmwáana íkárámu (Kimenyi 1978)
girl 3S PST give ASP child pen
"The girl gave the pen to the child."

b. *n-umukoòbwa* y-a-haá-ye úmwáana íkárámu
CFM girl 3S PST give ASP child pen
"It is the girl who gave the pen to the child."

c. *n-'iíkárámu* umukoòbwa y-a-haá- ye úmwáana
CFM pen girl 3S PST REL = give ASP child
"It is the pen that the girl gave (to) the child."

d. *n-uúmwáana* umukoòbwa y-a-haá -ye íkárámu
CFM child girl 3s PST REL = give ASP pen
"It is the child that the girl gave the pen (to)."

Compared with the corresponding non-cleft (61a), (61b) has a clefted subject, (61c) a clefted direct object, and (61d) a clefted indirect object. In all the cases, the cleft focus occurs initially, marked by the CFM *n-* and coindexed with a gap in the presupposed part of the sentence.

When oblique NPs are clefted, as in (62a), the NP together with its governing preposition must occur in sentence-initial position without leaving the preposition behind. Preposition stranding would not account for this, since (62b) is rejected where a resumptive pronoun *cyo* occurs after the preposition:

(62) a. *ni n-'íícyúuma* umubooyi a-kát -a inyama
CFM with-knife cook 3S REL = cut ASP meat
"It is the knife with which the cook is cutting the meat."

b. * *n- 'íícyúuma* umubooyi a-kát -a inyama ná (**cyo**)
CFM knife cook 3S REL = cut ASP meat with it

Genitive NPs are not cleftable at all in this pattern, whether the governing preposition is in focus position, as in (63a), or occurs in its underlying position with a resumptive pronoun, as in (63b):

(63) a. * *ni cy'ùmukoòbwa* umuhuùngu y-a-sóm -ye igitabo
CFM of-girl boy 3S PST REL = read ASP book
"It is the girl whose book the boy read."

b. * *n-uumukoòbwa* umuhuùngu y-a-sóm -ye igitabo cya (**e**)
CFM girl boy 3S PST REL = read ASP book of 3S

Cleft 2, on the other hand, is used in answer to *which*-questions, and differs structurally from Cleft 1 in that the focus part consists of a focused NP followed by the CFM *ni* plus a pronoun coreferential with the focused NP. This pronoun is obviously not part of the presupposed clause, given the fact that it is separated from the clause by a relative marker. (64) is a formal representation of the Cleft 2 construction:

(64) F_i CFM pro_i $[_{S'}$ REL $[_S \ldots e_i \ldots]]$

Cleft 2 is more restrictive in that only subjects and direct objects can be thus clefted. To wit,

(65) a. ábáana *ní bo* b-a-cií -ye igitabo
children CFM them 3PL PST REL = tear ASP book
"The children, it is they who tore up the book."

b. igitabo *ní cyo* ábáana b-a-cií -ye
book CFM it children 3PL PST REL = tear ASP
"The book, it is it that the children tore up."

The initial NP in (65a-b) may be analyzed as topic, followed by a cleft focus structure (Kimenyi 1978). The topic is recapitulated by the pronoun in focus, as evidenced by the linear order between the CFM and the pronoun. Thus Cleft 2 in fact contrastively focuses on a topicalized NP, a more complex construction than Cleft 1.

Since only subjects and direct objects, but not indirect objects or oblique NPs, can be clefted with Cleft 2, by (17c), the former must be more cleftable than all other NP positions on the Cleftability Hierarchy as far as Kinyarwanda data is concerned.

Cleftability in Kinyarwanda with regard to different NP positions is summarized in Table 2.7, which can be interpreted as:

SU = DO > IO = OBL > GEN.

The results, then, support the proposed Cleftability Hierarchy.

Table 2.7 ***Cleftability in Kinyarwanda***

	SU	DO	IO	OBL	GEN
Cleft 1	+	+	+	+	–
Cleft 2	+	+	–	–	–

2.4.5 Tera

Tera, like other Biu-Mandara languages of the Chadic language family, has a basic SVO order. The issue involved here is difference in cleftability between subjects and adverbials of time and location. Although cleftability of non-NPs will not be dealt with until Chapter 4, a discussion of Tera clefts here would shed further light on the criterion concerned.

2.4.5.1 The cleft construction

In Tera clefts, the focused constituent occurs initially and is marked by the CFM *ke*, which immediately follows the focus. For example,

(66) a. Ali kudir -a
Ali chief the
"Ali is the chief."

b. *Ali ke* kudir -a
Ali CFM chief the
"It is Ali who is the chief."

One might argue that the structure could be alternatively analyzed as involving no dislocation, but rather that the focus is marked solely by the CFM. In other words, from (66) alone, it is not clear whether the subject NP has a dependency relationship relating two positions; or the structure results from the mere insertion of a CFM after the focus constituent. However, sentences like (67) provide evidence for the dependency analysis against the simplex analysis:

(67) *Na ke* nàN kəs yurvu ba (Newman 1970:93)
I CFM I catch fish not
"It is I who didn't catch fish."

According to Newman (1970: 93), emphatic sentences, questions and relative clauses in Tera all have a reduced NP within the presupposed clause that agrees in person and number with the left-dislocated constituent. In (67), this is *nàN*, a kind of resumptive pronoun whose presence is obligatory when its antecedent is a pronoun (p. 91). In a simplex structure, the presence of this independent pronoun is totally superfluous and unaccounted for. On the other hand, if we posit an extra-sentential position for the cleft focus, the second pronoun will be a resumptive pronoun within the presupposed clause, and no such problem exists. Thus, the presence of two coindexed pronouns in (67) suggests that the focused subject has been left-dislocated.

Further evidence in support of this analysis is seen from non-subject clefting, where the focus is clearly dislocated:

(68) a. nàN ᴛwa'd Dala b'a
I beat Dala not
"I didn't beat Dala."

b. *Dala ke* nàN ᴛwatə nda b'a (Newman 1970:88)
Dala CFM I beat 3S not
"It is Dala that I didn't beat."

In (68b), the focused constituent, which is the underlying direct object, is fronted to the preverbal position and marked by *ke*, leaving behind a resumptive pronoun, *nda*, in its underlying position. It is obvious, therefore, that dislocation is involved in clefting in Tera.

2.4.5.2 Cleftability

Comparing (68b) with (66b), we notice that while (68b), with a clefted direct object, uses a resumptive pronoun, (66b), in which the subject is clefted, does not. The difference can be viewed as application of different strategies associated with clefting: pronoun deletion with clefted subjects, but pronoun retention with clefted direct objects. This discrepancy is predicted and accounted for by (17b) in the sense that pronoun deletion is associated with more accessible constituents while pronoun retention, with less accessible ones.

The picture that subject clefting and direct object clefting use distinct strategies is complicated by (69), where the direct object is clefted without a resumptive pronoun:

(69) *Dala ke* nàN ʇwad ba (Newman 1970:94)
Dala CFM I beat not
"It is Dala that I didn't beat."

(69) is simply an alternative to (68b). To accommodate this fact, let's state that while subjects in Tera are clefted via pronoun deletion only, objects are clefted via either pronoun deletion or pronoun retention. However, this complication does not weaken our position, in the sense that, measured against (17b), the fact that subject clefting does not allow for pronoun retention while object clefting does indeed lends support to the Cleftability Hierarchy hypothesis.

An apparent problem for the above analysis is seen in (67), in which a resumptive pronoun is retained after the subject is clefted. It seems that subject clefting, like direct object clefting, uses either the deletion or the retention strategy. However, we notice that the focused element in (67) is not a full NP but a pronoun, which somehow always requires an undeletable pronominal copy when clefted, irrespective of which grammatical function it has (Newman 1970: 91,93). It seems that we can treat sentences like (67) as a marked class and dismiss them as irrelevant to our consideration of cleftability in terms of syntactic positions. This is supported by the fact that if we substitute the pronoun subject with a full NP, we will have to use the deletion strategy, as in (70):

(70) *Ali ke* nə kəs yurvu ba (Newman 1970:93)
Ali CFM NEG = PERF catch fish not
"It is Ali who didn't catch fish."

As for indirect object clefting and oblique NP clefting, consider the following possible sentences in Tera:

(71) a. *woy ke* Ali vər ki goro ye * (**nda**)
boy CFM Ali give EMPH kola to 3s
"It is the boy that Ali gave kola to."

b. *woy ke* Ali də ki she * (**nda**)
boy CFM Ali go EMPH to 3s
"It is the boy that Ali went to."

Dative NPs and oblique NPs such as those exemplified herein, when clefted, obligatorily leave behind an assumptive pronoun after being left-dislocated. In other words, only the retention strategy is allowed. Absence of the assumptive pronoun, as indicated by * ( ), would result in ungrammaticality.

Also, (72a-b) show the pattern for clefting of adverbials of time and location, whose unmarked position is postverbal:

(72) a. *mbəda* *kə* tem kərma ki mato-a
yesterday CFM we repair EMPH car the
"It is yesterday that we repaired the car."

b. *a fən* *ke* gomar -a na
where CFM market the Q
"Where is it that the market is?"

c. a fən gomar -a na
where market the Q
"Where is the market?"

Put simply, clefting of adverbial of time or location requires the use of the deletion strategy, as can be seen from the minimal pair involving (72b) and (72c), and does not allow for pronoun retention.

The clefting patterns discussed so far can be summarized as in Table 2.8, where indirect objects and oblique NPs are collapsed.

Table 2.8 ***The clefting patterns of different constituents in Tera***

	SU	DO	IO/OBL	$ADVL_{t/l}$
Deletion	+	+	−	+
Retention	−	+	+	−

Table 2.8 shows that according to (17b), subjects and adverbials (of time or location), both using the deletion strategy in exclusion of the retention strategy, are most cleftable, followed by direct objects, whose clefting allows for either strategy. Direct objects are in turn followed by the collapsed indirect objects/oblique NPs, which allow for pronoun retention but not deletion. This can be interpreted and represented as: Sub = $ADVL_{t/l}$ > DO > IO/OBL, which conforms to the proposed Cleftability Hierarchy.

2.4.5.3 Distributions of SU and ADVL as cleft focus

As far as Table 2.8 is concerned, subjects and adverbials of time or location show no difference in cleftability. However, as (17c) indicates, it is possible sometimes to compare cleftability of different constituents by clefting them in more complex constructions which are usually considered "unpenetratable" by certain syntactic operations. Tera provides just such an example.

In addition to left-dislocation, Tera has another right-dislocation clefting pattern in its Wuyo dialect whereby the subject of an embedded relative clause can be contrastively focused by adding a coreferential pronoun after the verbal emphatic marker *ki* at the end of the relative clause (Newman 1970: 101):

(73) a. ʃi nə ke tem ká zəm
thing REL REL we will eat
"the thing which we will eat"

b. ʃi nə ke *tem* ká zəm *ki* *-mi*
thing REL REL we will eat EMPH 1PL
"the thing which **we** (not others) will eat"

We note that in (73b), clefting affects a constituent within a relative clause. As has been much discussed in the literature, complex NPs containing a relative clause are one of the island constructions (Ross 1967) where syntactic operations are often blocked. Given such a construction, the Cleftability Hierarchy predicts that if any syntactic operation, in one way or another, can affect a constituent within a relative clause at all, it will affect the constituents higher on the Hierarchy if it affects those lower on it, or it will only affect the subject. In Tera, only subjects can be thus contrastively focused. Since this is not possible with adverbials of time/location, the difference in degree of cleftability between subjects and such adverbials can be seen as SU > ADVL, reflected through more complex structures like complex NPs.

2.5 Frequency of Occurrence: More Frequent Versus Less Frequent

If we look at cleftability as reflecting processing ease or difficulty, and processing as a gradient notion, the degree of processing difficulty in terms of clefting of different constituents may be reflected in the relative number of languages instantiating the clefting possibilities in question. Our theory predicts, for instance, that there are more languages capable of clefting SU than there are languages capable of clefting DO, etc., because "grammars will select the unmarked and more highly valued structures potentially available to them [e. g. SU in this case] before they resort to the more marked and less highly valued ones" (Hawkins 1988:22). The more highly valued options tend to be grammaticalized more frequently. Such frequency can be intralinguistic or crosslinguistic. Intralinguistic frequency is the ratio with which each syntactic position is clefted to the number of cleft sentences found in a corpus of a language, for example, the percentage of SU-clefting sentences in the total number of cleft sentences found in a text. Crosslinguistic frequency refers to the number of languages capable of clefting a certain position as against the number of languages capable of clefting another on the Cleftability Hierarchy. We will look at these two kinds of frequency in turn.

2.5.1 Intralinguistic frequency

Following Keenan's (1987b: 49) suggestion with respect to relativization, one way to discover difference in cleftability among different grammatical positions that appear to be equally cleftable in terms of grammaticality and clefting strategy is by comparing the frequency with which each position is clefted in natural texts. In English, for example, all cleftable positions are clefted with the deletion strategy, and appear equally grammatical, as in (74):

(74) a. It is John that came.
b. It is John that I saw.
c. It is John that she gave a book to.
d. It is John that she went to the movies with.
e. It is John whose car broke down.
f. It is John that Tom is taller than.

However, there are significant pragmatic differences among them in terms of frequency of occurrence in natural texts.

Such differences are reported in a corpus-based statistical study of English cleft sentences (Collins 1987, 1991), in which data from the London_Lund and LOB corpora are analyzed and percentages of cleft sentences with different clefted constituents are calculated against a total number of 752 cleft sentences found in the texts. Though no statistical test other than the frequency count was used, the results in terms of percentage of each occurring category against the total number of cleft sentences found clearly present supporting evidence for the Cleftability Hierarchy. Table 2.9 is adapted from Collins' Table 5 (p. 13), and has reordered the cleftable positions and omitted irrelevant details.

In Table 2.9, we find that in terms of grammatical positions, subjects are the most frequently clefted (38.3%), closed followed by adverbials (36.7%), which are usually realized by PPs or adverbial clauses. DO-clefts lag far behind (7.2%), and IO/Obl with their combined forces are only about half as frequent as DO-clefts (3.2%). No percentage of clefted genitive NPs and OComp is reported, probably either because these are not attested or because they were not taken into consideration in the original study. The difference in percentage between subject clefting and adverbial clefting, given the close range, is probably not significant. Figure 2.1 graphically re-presents the relative frequencies of the grammatical functions clefted.

Table 2.9 ***Comparison of frequency of occurrence among cleftable constituents in English texts*** (adapted from Collins 1987)

Grammatical Position	Number	Percentage
SUB	288	38.3%
ADVL	276	36.7%
(zero)	109	14.5%
DO	54	7.2%
IO/OBL	24	3.2%
Sub Compl	1	0.1%
TOTAL	752	100%

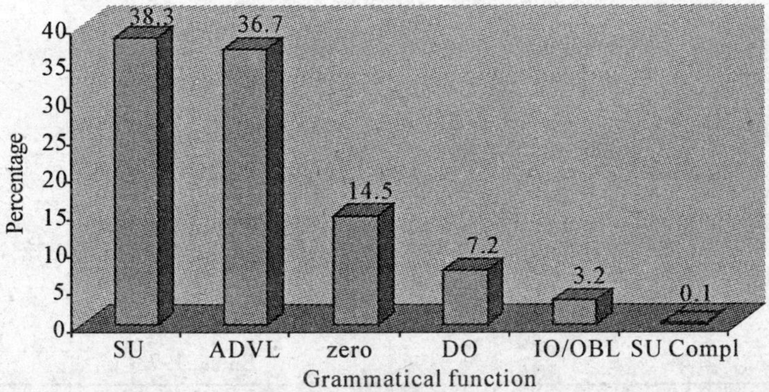

Figure 2.1 *Cleftability in English Texts: Intralinguistic Frequency* (%)

According to the attested frequencies, we can rank the clefted constituents along the scale: SUB > ADVL > DO > IO/OBL, which corresponds to the ordering of positions on the Cleftability Hierarchy except the ADVL, whose high cleftability is to be discussed in Chapter 5.

2.5.2 Crosslinguistic frequency

As defined above, crosslinguistic frequency refers to the number of languages capable of clefting a certain position as against the number of languages capable of clefting another on the Cleftability Hierarchy. While a more exhaustive study for collecting and analyzing crosslinguistic data which reflects such frequency is beyond the scope of the present study, crosslinguistic data from 40 languages is surveyed and analyzed in terms of attested relative frequency of occurrence of each position on the Cleftability Hierarchy. Table 2. 10 summarizes, and Figure 2. 2 graphically represents, such crosslinguistic frequency of cleftability of various grammatical positions on the Cleftability Hierarchy, as attested in the various languages surveyed.

Table 2. 10 ***Crosslinguistic frequency of cleftability of grammatical functions***

Language	SU	DO	IO	OBL	GEN	Advl	Sources
Bade	+						Schuh 1971
Basque	+	+					Saltarelli et al. 1988
Berber	+	+	+	+		+	Ennaji & Sadiqi 1986
Breton	+	+				+	Timm 1987
Chinese	+		+	+		+	Huang 1982; Ross 1983; my data
Danish	+	+			$+_{su}$	+	Smits 1989
Dera	+						Schuh 1971
Dutch	+	+	+	+	+	+	Smits 1989
English	+	+	+	+	+	+	*ibid.*
French	+	+			$+_{do}$	+	*ibid.*
German	+	+	+	+	+	+	*ibid.*
Icelandic	+	+				+	*ibid.*
Indonesian	+						Chung 1978

continuous

Language	SU	DO	IO	OBL	GEN	Advl	Sources
Irish	+	+	+	+		+	McCloskey 1979
Ivatan	+	+					Reid 1966
Italian	+	+	+	+	+	+	Smits 1989
Kanuri	+	+				+	Lukas 1967
Karekare	+						Schuh 1971
Kihung'an	+	+					Takizala 1973
Kinyarwanda	+	+	+	+		+	Kimenyi 1978
Kpelle	+	+		+		+	Welmers 1964
Malagasy	+					+	Keenan 1985; Harries-D 1978
Malay	+	+	+			+	my data
Maori	+	+					Chung 1978
Margi	+						Hoffmann 1966
Ngizim	+						Schuh 1971
Norwegian	+	+		+		+	Smits 1989
Pukapukan	+	+	+	+		+	Chung 1978
Rennellese	+	+	+	+		+	*ibid.*
Samoan	+	+	+	+		+	*ibid.*
Somali	+	+				+	Bell 1953
Swedish	+	+	+		+	+	Smits 1989
Taba-Batak	+						Percival 1981
Temne	+	+	+				Nemer 1987
Tera	+	+	+	+		+	Newman 1970
Tojolabal	+	+					Brody 1984
Tongan	+	+	+	+			Chung 1978
Welsh	+	+				+	Dik 1980
Yapese	+	+				+	Jensen 1977
Yoruba	+	+		+	+	+	Bamgbose 1966
Total	40	31	16	16	8	27	
% (N=40)	100	77.5	40	40	20	**67.5**	

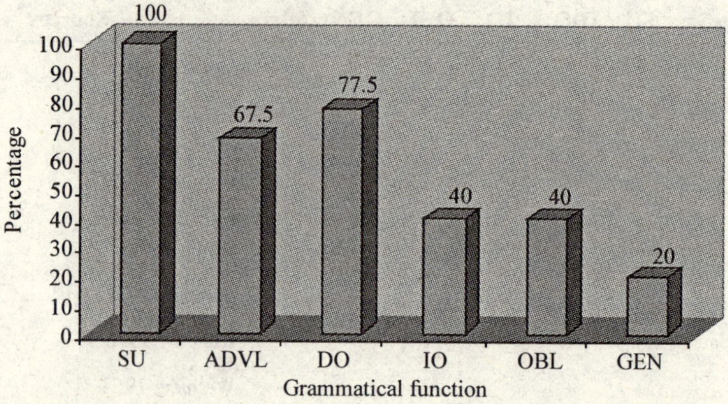

Note: The percentage shows the proportion of all languages under study which allow a given grammatical function to be clefted.

Figure 2.2 *Cleftability of Grammatical Functions: Crosslinguistic Frequency* (%)

In Table 2.10, subject (SU) has been realigned with S and P, and direct object (DO), with A, in syntactically ergative languages. The reason for the adjustment is to be detailed in 3.1. Suffice it to say now that such adjustment is in line with the need to reinterpret transitive subjects and direct objects in analyzing ergative languages. Also, for languages where indirect objects (IO) and oblique objects (OBL) are collapsed, separate frequency counts were made of each for statistical purposes, which presumably will not affect the frequency counting significantly. In terms of clefting strategy, a constituent is considered cleftable if it can be clefted through either the deletion or retention strategy. Finally, a position is deemed cleftable in a particular language only if a cleft sentence with a constituent in that position clefted is fully grammatical, thus excluding instances with questionable grammaticality.

In terms of the NP positions on the Cleftability Hierarchy, the results show that crosslinguistic frequency supports the proposed Hierarchy. In a descending order, SU is found cleftable in all 40 languages (100%); and DO, in 31 of them (77.5%). No significant difference is found between IO, in 16 languages (40%), and OBL, in 16 languages (40%), which does not affect the validity of the Cleftability Hierarchy. GEN is found to be cleftable in only 8 languages (20%). Finally, OComp clefting is not attested, given lack of examples thereof①. Therefore, in terms of crosslinguistic frequency, the order of the positions attested can be shown as:

SU > DO > IO = OBL > GEN,

which corresponds to the order on the Cleftability Hierarchy except the above-mentioned non-distinctiveness between IO and OBL. Thus, the Cleftability Hierarchy is further supported by both intralinguistic and crosslinguistic frequency of occurrence.

To facilitate discussion on high cleftability of adverbials in both Chapter 4 and Chapter 5, the frequency of occurrence of clefted adverbials is also given in Table 2.10 in comparison to clefted NPs. Following Delahunty (1984), such adverbials include adverbial PPs, NPs and clauses. The results show that adverbial clefting is ranked third (67.5%), after subjects (100%) and direct objects (77.5%). Compared with Table 2.9 on intralinguistic frequency (2.5.1) where adverbial clefting (36.7%) is far more frequent than DO clefting (7.2%), Table 2.10 shows that DO clefting is slightly more frequent than adverbial clefting. Despite this discrepancy between intralinguistic frequency of occurrence based on corpus analysis (Table 2.9) and crosslinguistic frequency based on grammatical possibilities (Table 2.10), adverbial clefting has been shown to enjoy high cleftability crosslinguistically.

2.6 Promotion to Higher Positions for Clefting

So far we have examined crosslinguistic data against the criteria set forth in (17a-d), and can reach a tentative conclusion that the Cleftability Hierarchy is supported by rather strong empirical evidence. To further strengthen this position, let us look at some other independent evidence.

One kind of such evidence can be found in syntactic processes which promote certain constituents to higher positions on the Accessibility Hierarchy for various purposes. Application of different clefting strategies, as mentioned earlier, can be perceived as relevant to the cleftability of a given constituent. For example, pronoun retention is said to help make an NP lower on the Cleftability Hierarchy more accessible to clefting. Some languages, however, have recourse to another way of

① However, grammaticality judgement shows that English allows OComp clefting, as has been mentioned in the literature and the above discussion.

increasing cleftability of such NPs, *viz.* by promoting them to higher positions on the Hierarchy. Usually, such an NP is promoted through the process of subjectivization by way of detransitivization or passivization, or through objectivization. Support for such promotion for clefting is found in Indonesian for subjectivization and Kinyarwanda for objectivization.

2.6.1 Subjectivization in Indonesian

As mentioned in 2.2.1.3, clefting in formal Indonesian, as in many other Western Austronesian languages, is restricted to subjects only. The focused NP is left-dislocated with the deletion strategy, and no CFM is present. Direct objects as a rule cannot be thus clefted, as seen in (26), reproduced here as (75b):

(75) a. dokter itu me-meriksa saya
doctor the TRANS-examine 1s
"The doctor examined me."

b. * *saya* yang dokter itu me-meriksa
1s COMP doctor the TRANS-examine
"It was me that the doctor examined."

However, an underlying direct object *can* be clefted by being first promoted to subject through passivization if the underlying subject is a common noun or through object-preposing and verb detransitivizing if the underlying subject is a pronoun or a proper noun (Chung 1978:371). For example, if the underlying subject is a pronoun, the underlying direct object can be preposed to become a derived subject, with the underlying subject now encliticized to the left of the verb and the transitive prefix dropped.

(76) a. saya me-meriksa dokter itu
1s TRANS-examine doctor the
"I examined the doctor."

b. dokter itu saya periksa
doctor the 1S examine
"I examined the doctor / The doctor was examined by me."

c. *dokter itu* yang saya periksa (Chung 1978: 370-1)
doctor the COMP 1S examine
"It was the doctor that I examined."

Compared with the unmarked (76a), (72b) involves a preposed (i.e. subjectivized) direct object (i. e. *dokter itu* "the doctor") and a detransitivized verb (*periksa* "examine"). The underlying subject, *saya* "I", is demoted and appears as an enclitic to the left of the detransitivized verb. Now that the underlying direct object has become a derived subject, it can be clefted, as in (76c). Since an uncleftable DO can be clefted if it assumes the subject status in some way but not vice versa, subjects are shown to be more cleftable than direct objects, as predicted by (17e).

2.6.2 Objectivization in Kinyarwanda

A similar process is found in derived objects in Kinyarwanda. To recapitulate, we have seen in 2.4.4 that in Kinyarwanda, subjects, direct objects, indirect objects and oblique NPs are all cleftable with the Cleft 1 pattern, but not genitive NPs. However, a genitive NP may be promoted by virtue of losing its genitive marking (and the accompanying change of the verb marking accordingly), similar to the loss of the transitive verbal prefix in Indonesian. The effect of this is that the genitive NP now appears more like an unmarked direct object and can be so treated, which is seen in the fact that it now can be clefted in the same way as a direct object is. Thus, compare (77) with (78):

(77) *n-uumukoòbwa* umuhuùngu y-a-sóm-e-ye igitabo
CFM- girl boy 3S-PST-REL = read-APPL-ASP book
"It is the girl whose book the boy read."

(78) a. ∗ *ni cy'ùmukoòbwa* umuhuùngu y-a-sóm-ye igitabo
CFM of-girl boy 3S-PST-REL = read-ASP book
"It is the girl whose book the boy read."

b. ∗ *n-uumukoòbwa* umuhuùngu y-a-sóm-ye igitabo **cya** (e)
CFM- girl boy 3S-PST-REL = read-ASP book of 3S
"It is the girl whose book the boy read."

The crucial difference between (77) and (78) is that in (78a) or (78b), there is a genitive marker, *cya*, which is dropped in (77). With the dropping of the genitive marker, the genitive NP now becomes object-like, and (77) now structurally resembles (79) in which a direct object is clefted:

(79) *n-'ìíkárámu* umukoòbwa y-a-haá-ye úmwáana
CFM- pen girl 3S PST REL = give ASP child
"It is the pen that the girl gave (to) the child."

Thus, once promoted to object, a constituent low on the Cleftability Hierarchy can acquire higher cleftability.

Examples like these provide further independent evidence to the Cleftability Hierarchy, in the sense that subjectivization or objectivization are independently motivated; for example, they may be motivated by reasons similar to those for antipassivization, or they may exist independently as a fact of morphological marking (as in Pukapukan 3.1.2). However, once a constituent that is uncleftable or low in cleftability is so promoted, its cleftability increases, which is convincing evidence for the validity of the Cleftability Hierarchy.

2.7 Diachronic Precedence: Indonesian

Apart from what has been said about Indonesian, the language also provides some evidence for the proposed Cleftability Hierarchy in terms of language change. The assumption taken here is that language change can be reflected in different patterns of cleftability with regard to various syntactic positions. More specifically, as a result of such changes, some previously uncleftable positions may become cleftable. However, change in the cleftability pattern is not random, but constrained by the CH in the following way:

(80) **Diachronically, linguistic change will not break up continuous segments of the Cleftability Hierarchy.**

In other words, the CH predicts that, if there is a change in the cleftability pattern across constituents which renders a previously uncleftable constituent cleftable, then the affected constituent must not be separated on the Hierarchy from other already cleftable constituent(s) by an uncleftable one. For example, if a language has a previously uncleftable constituent, say, DO, which now becomes cleftable as a result of language change, then it must be the case that the language must have a previously cleftable subject but not a previously cleftable oblique NP. Looking from a different angle, if a language has previously cleftable subjects and previously uncleftable direct objects and indirect objects, (17f) predicts that it is direct objects that will become cleftable if language change makes cleftable one of the previously uncleftable positions.

Theoretically, such changes can be detected, among other things, in languages with a very conservative grammar and a concurrent innovative one which provide basis for comparison. Comparison between the two systems in terms of the same grammatical phenomenon can often reveal tendencies of language change.

As pointed by Chung (1978), Indonesian is such a language in which we can compare a very prescriptive grammar with its more innovative colloquial version, a comparison which reflects, among other things, change in cleftability patterns.

In formal Indonesian, as described in 2.2.1.3, clefting is restricted to subjects only, and direct objects are generally not cleftable. However, underlying direct objects can be clefted if only they are derived subjects, either by way of passivization if the underlying subject of the clause is a common noun, or by way of object preposing if the underlying subject is a pronoun or proper noun, as shown in 2.6.1. Either way, formal Indonesian is seen as allowing only subjects (underlying or derived) to be clefted.

Colloquial Indonesian, on the other hand, allows for direct object as well as subject clefting. Consider (76b) again, reproduced here as (81):

(81) *dokter itu yang* saya periksa
doctor the COMP I examine
"It was the doctor that I examined."

According to Chung (1978: 372), cleft sentences like (81), which in formal Indonesian are derived from the underlying structure (83) through object preposing, should be considered as deriving directly from underlying structures like (82) in colloquial Indonesian, in which no transitive verb prefix is used in canonical transitive clauses:

(82) saya periksa dokter itu (colloquial Indonesian)
1s examine doctor the
"I examined the doctor."

(83) saya me-meriksa dokter itu (formal Indonesian)
1s TRANS-examine doctor the
"I examined the doctor."

The direct derivation position is supported by the fact that not only sentences whose underlying subjects are pronouns or proper nouns, but also those with common noun subjects, can cleft direct objects through object-preposing. As noted in 2.6.1, object-preposing applies only when the underlying subject is a pronoun or proper noun but not a common noun. In other words, underlying common noun subjects prevent direct objects from being preposed in formal Indonesian. The fact that in colloquial Indonesian, direct objects *can* indeed occur in initial position as clefted foci irrespective of the type of underlying subject, as shown in (84), which has a underlying common noun subject, suggests the innovation in colloquial Indonesian that clefted DO's are derived directly from underlying DO's without an intermediate stage of object-preposing.

(84) *hanya nama itu saja yang* tukang beca tahu (Dyen 1964: 19)
only name the just COMP worker pedicab know
"It is only this name that the pedicab driver knows."

In sum, formal Indonesian allows only for subject clefting, whereas colloquial Indonesian allows both subject and direct object to be clefted. Given that the former tends to reflect more conservative use of the language and the latter more innovative use, cleftability in Indonesian is probably being extended from subject only to subject *and* direct object. This development is consistent with (80), which asserts that diachronic change will not break up continuous segments of the Cleftability Hierarchy. The fact that in Indonesian it is the DO but not any oblique NP that has been found to be cleftable in colloquial use, (which would have left DO an uncleftable discontinuous gap on the CH,) lends further support to the proposed Cleftability Hierarchy.

Chapter 3 NP Cleftability—Counterevidence?

This chapter continues to examine cleftability of NPs in terms of two kinds of apparent counterevidence, both relating to DO cleftability and both revealing interesting interactions between the Cleftability Hierarchy and other parts of grammar in a language. The first kind of apparent counterexample concerns relative cleftability of transitive subjects and direct objects in syntactically ergative languages such as Eastern Austronesian languages. The second kind of apparent counterexample concerns DO uncleftability in Chinese and shows interaction between the Cleftability Hierarchy and language specific constraints.

3.1 Cleftability and Ergativity

Crosslinguistic data, when closely examined, sometimes reveals recurring patterns apparently contrary to the Cleftability Hierarchy. One such type of counterevidence worth noting involves examples which show, according to our criteria, greater direct object cleftability than transitive subject cleftability in syntactically ergative languages. A preliminary account for such typologically different sentences has been given in 2.3.1.2 to show that such counterexamples are apparent than real, and they do not really invalidate the Cleftability Hierarchy. A closer scrutiny of additional data from several languages will be given below, followed by a more elaborated theoretical discussion on the nature of the problem as well as how to deal with it.

3.1.1 Mayan languages

According to the Accessibility Hierarchy, (1), subjects in different languages should be more accessible to relativization or clefting than direct objects. However, in many syntactically ergative languages in which S and P are treated alike and A, differently, ergative subject NPs may not as a rule be clefted nor relativized, while absolutive NPs can (Shaumyan 1985). In order for an ergative NP to be relativizable or cleftable, it must, for example, first become an absolutive NP by virtue of the verb being antipassivized with a special detransitivizing suffix, as is the case with relativization in Dyirbal (Dixon 1979). For clefting, consider (85) from Quiche, a Mayan language:

(85) a. *aree lee achih* x-Ø-ch'ay-**ow** lee ixoq (Shaumyan 1985)
CFM the man COMP-3SA-hit-DETRANS the woman
"It was the man who hit the woman."

b. *aree lee ixoq* x-Ø-**u**-ch'ay lee achih
CFM the woman COMP-3SA-hit the man
"It was the woman that the man hit."

In (85), the detransitivizing suffix *-ow* is added to facilitate clefting of the ergative NP. As a result of this detransitivization, the ergative subject agreement prefix, *u-*, required in a declarative matrix sentence, now disappears from the verb stem. Another Mayan language, Aguacatec, presents a similar case (Larsen & Norman 1979):

(86) a. ja Ø-Ø-b'iy yaaj xna^{7}n
ASP 3SA-3SE-hit man woman
"The man hit the woman."

b. *yaaj* m-Ø-b'iy-**oon** xna^{7}n
man DES. ASP-3SA-hit-DETRANS woman
"It was the man who hit the woman."

In (86b), the ergative subject prefix disappears from the verb stem, and the detransitivizing suffix *-oon* is added for the ergative subject to be clefted. The Aguacatec cleft sentence differs from its Quiche counterpart in that there is neither a focus marker nor a complementizer in (86b).

In contrast to ergative NP clefting, clefting of an absolutive NP follows the normal pattern without any difficulty. For example, in (85b), where the direct object is clefted, there is no subsequent change in the verb stem: the ergative subject agreement prefix remains intact and no detransitivizing suffix is added.

3.1.2 Pukapukan

Pukapukan is a Samoic-Outlier language of the Polynesian family, with a basic

VSO order. It has a mixed accusative-ergative case system (Chung 1978:61) in which it allows "accusative", "ergative" and "passive" case marking for underlyingly transitive clauses. The three patterns appear to vary rather freely with basic transitive sentences; the only difference seems to be one of register: accusative patterns used in formal, polite language; the ergative in informal, casual registers; and the passive in neutral registers. However, when it comes to sentences with unbounded dependencies such as clefts and questions, the variation is not as free.

The case-marking systems are summarized in Table 3.1.

Table 3.1 ***Case marking systems in Pukapukan***

	TRANSITIVE			INTRANSITIVE
	SU	DO	V-sfx	SU
Accusative	Ø	i	Ø	Ø*
Passive	e	Ø	-Cia	
Ergative	e	Ø	Ø	

* When an intransitive subject is a proper noun or 3sg pronoun marked by a preceding article *a*-, the nominative marker is *i*, a case where S is as marked as P.

Clefting moves a focused NP to the left and marks it with the CFM *ko*. In terms of clefting strategies, deletion is limited to subjects only, affecting both intransitive subjects (87a) and transitive subjects in the accusative pattern (87b-c).

(87) a. *ko* *Yinaliulu* ya tu i te uluulu akau
CFM Yinaliulu PST stand at the outer = reef
"It was Yinaliulu who was standing on the outer reef."

b. *ko-na* na tuku **i** te kou
CFM-he PST give ACC the gift
"It is he who gave the present."

c. *ko* *te* *toa* na patu **i** te wawine
CFM the warrior PST hit ACC the woman
"It is the warrior who hit the woman."

Accusative direct objects or oblique NPs, on the other hand, can not be clefted via the deletion strategy; pronoun retention is required instead. Thus, a pronoun, *ai*, appears in (88a-c):

(88) a. *ko te wawine* na patu te toa **ai**
CFM the woman PST hit the warrior PRO
"It is the woman that the warrior hit."

b. *ko te moana* na yi-ika **ai** latou
CFM the ocean PST catch-fish PRO they
"It is the ocean that they were fishing in."

c. *ko te tane* na maua **ai** te wua lakau
CFM the man PST caught PRO the egg tree
"It is the man because of whom the fruit was gotten."

For the ergative pattern, the unmarked NP (= P) can always be clefted via deletion, just like the subject in the accusative pattern. This is shown in (89a-b), where no resumptive pronoun is used when an absolutive NP, in this case the direct object, is clefted:

(89) a. *ko te wawa* ka tunu e te tama
CFM the taro FUT cook ERG the boy
"It is the taro that the boy is about to cook."

b. *ko Uyo* la kiai la na maua ete patu e te wenua
CFM Uyo that not that PST able COMP kill ERG the island
"It was Uyo who the (island) people were unable to kill."

The ergative NP(= A), on the other hand, is only marginally cleftable via the deletion strategy:

(90) a. ? *ko te toa* na patu te tamaiti
CFM the warrior PST hit the child
"It is the warrior who hit the child."

b. ? *ko te Malo* kiai na pepelu te malo
CFM Te Malo not PST don the loincloth
"It is Te Malo who did not don the loincloth."

In Pukapukan, then, it is possible to compare accusative clefting and ergative clefting. While the former is in line with the CH, the latter presents more difficulty with transitive subject clefting than with direct object clefting. More specifically, it is more difficult to cleft an ergative subject via deletion than an absolutive object. This appears contrary to what the proposed CH predicts.

3.1.3 Subject reinterpreted

The fact that direct objects in the aforementioned Polynesian as well as Mayan languages are more accessible than (ergative) subjects poses a challenge for the proposed Cleftability Hierarchy as a putative universal. To solve this problem, we can either declare the inadequacy of the CH, or reinterpret the concept *subject* so that absolutive NPs can be treated as subjects. Since the former solution is undesirably simplistic before other possibilities are exhausted, rather than quickly dismiss the CH as untenable, the latter alternative will be examined by proposing a solution by reinterpreting subject and object in ergative patterns, so that absolutive NPs can be reinterpreted as SUs and ergative NPs as DOs.

It should be noted that reinterpretation of subjects relies crucially on the relationship between morphological ergativity and syntactic ergativity, regarding which two opposing views have been expressed, *viz.* the Integrated Position and the Independent Position. According to the Integrated Position, the categories picked out by the case marking of a language are the same categories that its syntactic rules refer to, i.e. the syntax of every language should parallel its morphology. For example, morphologically accusative languages should not exhibit syntactic ergativity, and morphologically ergative languages should not exhibit syntactic nominativity. According to the Independent Position (Anderson 1976, Perlmutter & Postal 1974), the categories picked out by the case marking of a language need not be the same as those that its syntactic rules refer to. Therefore, a language's syntax and its morphology may be organized differently, such that a morphologically ergative language may turn out to be syntactically accusative. Studies of the world's languages have provided syntactic facts against the Integrated Position in favour of the Independent Position. For example, subject-referring rules such as Clitic Placement, Equi-NP Deletion and Raising exist in ergative languages such as Tongan and Samoan (Chung 1978), both being Austronesian languages, and Basque (2.2.2.1) offers an example of morphological ergativity versus syntactic accusativity.

Taking the Independent Position in characterizing syntactic ergativity and accusativity, Comrie (1978) defines subjects as follows:

> if in a language S and A are regularly identified, that is, if the language is consistently or overwhelmingly nominative-accusative, then we are justified in

> using the term *subject* to group together S and A; if in a language S and P are regularly identified (consistent or overwhelming ergative-absolutive system), then we would be justified in using the term *subject* rather to refer to S and P.

According to this view, a transitive subject (A) has the same grammatical status as the intransitive subject (S) in accusative languages, and an absolutive object (P) should be treated grammatically like an intransitive subject (S) in ergative languages.

This analysis is supported by the following argument. The grammatical relations *subject* and *direct object* do not have single, universal definitions applicable to every language (Schachter 1976, 1977; Foley and Van Valin 1977; Gil 1984). Instead, the various grammatical relations may be defined in terms of clusters of properties (Keenan 1976[87]). Thus, an NP is a SU or a DO to the extent that it exhibits a specific array of SU or DO properties.

As Comrie (1988) points out, in general, it is uncontroversial that the single argument of an intransitive predicate (S) is the SU of that predicate. Therefore, to say that some argument of a transitive predicate is SU of its clause is to claim that it shares properties with SUs of intransitive clauses. In English, S and A are grouped together insofar as they share SU properties such as nominative case, triggering verb agreement, being the trigger and target for conjunction reduction, and control. In languages exhibiting ergativity, at least some properties are common to P and S, although languages vary as to the extent of such shared properties. A fairly extreme example is Dyirbal (Dixon 1979), where most relevant SU properties are shared by P and not A (Comrie 1988; Faarlund 1988).

Typical DO properties, among other things, include lesser referential strength and indefiniteness (Givon 1984; Gil 1984). However, these properties are not exhibited by P in many ergative languages. In Tagalog, for example, patient NPs do not show low referentiality; in fact, patients are more strongly referential than actors/agents and are generally interpreted as definite. Both properties point to P as less DO-like and more SU-like. As Gil (1984:100) suggests, "quasi-subjects are like real subjects, except that they are actually more likely to be patients; similarly, quasi-direct-objects resemble *bona fide* direct objects, except that in basic sentences they are generally actors."

If, as the above argument suggests, it is indeed possible to reinterpret P as SU and A as DO in languages where syntactic rules consistently group S and P together, then to the extent that languages like Tongan and Pukapukan exhibit split ergativity in the use of clefting strategies, we may reinterpret the relationship as in (91), which, by providing a possible typological account for the cleftability patterns in languages like Tongan and Pukapukan, enables us to analyze data from such languages in line with the CH without encountering problems of the sort mentioned above, with the unmarked case being always more cleftable①:

(91)	CH:	SU	>	DO	> ...
	Accusative:	S, A		P	
	Ergative:	S, P		A	

Since S and P in ergative languages are like nominative NPs in accusative languages, just as A in ergative languages is like accusative NPs in accusative languages, the data presented in 3. 1. 2 actually supports, rather than rejects, the CH. Typologically, we can footnote the segment SU > DO on the Cleftability Hierarchy by stating that in syntactically ergative languages, SU should be interpreted as absolutive and DO as ergative, as shown in (91) above.

In conclusion, it has been shown that the deviations from the CH in terms of cleftability in several Mayan and Eastern Austronesian languages are due to two factors: transitivity and ergativity. Therefore, while the CH is independently verifiable in terms of clefting (Luo 1994), its interaction with transitivity and ergativity may result in cleftability patterns deviant from those predicted by the CH. Thus, an adequate description of cleftability needs to take into account the interaction between the CH and other parts of the grammar.

3.2 Cleftability and Language Specific Constraints: Chinese

Another kind of apparent counterevidence to the Cleftability Hierarchy (CH) can be represented by uncleftability of direct objects in Chinese. This section will address the issue in some detail, to see whether such apparent counterevidence really impairs the CH and, if not, what causes the inaccessibility of direct objects to clefting in Chinese, and possibly other languages.

① Further research is needed to find more evidence of syntactic ergativity in other constructions in these languages.

3.2.1 The problem of DO uncleftability

In Chinese, the cleft focus is marked by an immediately preceding contrastive focus marker① (CFM), *shi*, which is identical in form to the copula verb. In addition, a modifier marker②, *de* (Ross 1983), occurs toward the end of the cleft sentence, though sometimes optionally. No apparent dislocation is involved. This pattern is formally represented as (92), where F stands for the cleft focus, and X and Y, for any variables respectively.

(92) X *shi* F Y (*de*)

The cleft focus usually receives some extra stress, and can be almost any constituent on the CH except the direct object, as shown in (93).

(93) a. Zhang San cong guowai gei ta ji le xin.
Zhang San from abroad to 3S mail PERF letter
"Zhang San mailed a letter to him from abroad."
张三从国外给他寄了信。

b. *shi* **Zhang San** cong guowai gei ta ji xin de.
CFM Zhang San from abroad to 3S mail letter MM
"It is Zhang San who mailed a letter to him from abroad."
是张三从国外给他寄信的。

c. Zhang San cong guowai *shi* **gei ta** ji xin de.
Zhang San from abroad CFM to 3S mail letter MM
"It is to him that Zhang San mailed a letter from abroad."
张三从国外是给他寄信的。

d. Zhang San *shi* **cong guowai** gei ta ji xin de.
Zhang San CFM from abroad to 3S mail letter MM
"It is from abroad that Zhang San mailed a letter to him."
张三是从国外给他寄信的。

---

① While the working definition in this book is largely functional, Huang (1982a) argues, with particular reference to clefting, that languages like Chinese may involve movement in its LF component even if no movement is apparent in SS. Therefore, the term "cleft" is considered warranted here.

② This modifier marker (MM) is usually in complementary distribution with the perfective morpheme *-le*, as shown in later examples.

e. ＊Zhang San cong guowai gei ta ji *shi* **xin** de.
Zhang San from abroad to 3S mail CFM letter MM
"It is a letter that Zhang San mailed him from abroad."
＊张三从国外给他寄是信的。

While (93a) is a non-cleft with the basic proposition, (93b-d) respectively have as the cleft focus the subject (93b), the indirect object (93c), and an oblique object (93d)①. (93e), where the direct object is the cleft focus, is ruled as ungrammatical.

The uncleftability of direct objects in Chinese poses a problem for the CH: the fact that it is possible to cleft indirect objects and oblique objects but not direct objects contradicts the CH, which predicts just the opposite. This situation also results in a discontinuous segment on the CH in terms of the same clefting strategy, as in (94), a violation of the Continuity Constraint (15):

(94) SU ＊DO IO OBL (GEN)②

This problem of DO uncleftability was first recognized by Teng (1979:104) as "a perplexing problem", and was later on tackled briefly in Huang (1982), to whose account we will return in 3.2.3.

There are at least two approaches to this problem. One is to treat direct objects in Chinese as inherently inaccessible to clefting and claim the inapplicability of the CH to Chinese cleft sentences as exceptional. The other is to examine factors other than the direct object and the CH, and see how they interact with each other and affect cleftability. The first approach is less advisable for two reasons. First, to claim that the CH is not applicable to Chinese clefting is too simplistic and adversely affects universality of the CH. Secondly, if we look at accessibility of direct objects to other syntactic operations, we find that they are easily accessible to syntactic processes such as topicalization (95a), relativization (95b), question formation (95c), and pseudo-clefting (95d). To use a term from phonology, by pattern congruity, it is not

---

① Because Chinese, like many other languages, does not allow for preposition stranding, the CFM *shi* must precede the whole PP in focus. Since this is independent of cleftability in that a preverbal cleftable oblique NP becomes uncleftable once posposed, as will be dealt with later, the issue of preposition stranding will not be elaborated here.

② Clefting of GEN NP frequently involves long distance dependency relations and the pronoun retention strategy in Chinese. Therefore, it is less relevant here.

very plausible to claim that direct objects in Chinese are inherently inaccessible to clefting.

(95) a. shu wo yijing mai le.
book 1s already buy PERF
"The book, I already bought."
书我已经买了。

b. zhe shi wo mai de shu.
this is 1s buy MM book
"This is the book I bought."
这是我买的书。

c. ni mai le shenme?
2s buy PERF what
"What did you buy?"
你买了什么?

d. ta mai de shi shu.
3s buy NOM is book
"What he bought is a book."
他买的是书。

Given such facts, the first approach, by treating direct objects in Chinese as inherently inaccessible to clefting, would require an *ad hoc* statement on the inaccessibility of DO to clefting in Chinese, and therefore is less desirable if we can find non-*ad hoc* alternatives. In comparison, the second approach, as detailed below, does not necessarily require any *ad hoc* solution or impair universality of the CH.

Therefore, instead of simply discrediting the CH, the second approach will be adopted; and it will be contended that DO uncleftability in Chinese stems not from overgeneralization of the CH, but from a language-specific linear constraint in Chinese.

3.2.2 A linear constraint

Synchronically, Chinese has an unmarked order of SVO① (Sun & Givón 1985),

① On the other hand, Li and Thompson (1975) hold that Chinese is changing from an SVO to an SOV language. Despite the discrepant views, it is generally accepted that the direct object unmarkedly occurs after the verb in Chinese.

with direct objects unmarkedly occurring postverbally. Linearly, however, the contrastive focus marker (CFM), *shi*, must invariably occur before the main verb of the sentence. In other words, the CFM *shi* as a rule can not occur after the main verb. This constraint, implicitly stated in Huang (1982: 291), can be formally stated as (96):

(96) *X MV *shi* Y

(96) stipulates that no postverbal CFM is permitted in Chinese, which is potentially conflicting to (92), which states that the CFM must immediately precede the cleft focus. Now if we consider (92) and (96) in terms of word order in Chinese, DO uncleftability is accounted for: for a direct object, which occurs postverbally, to be clefted, the CFM must immediately precede it, resulting in a postverbal CFM *shi*, which violates (96).

The implications of (96), from the way it is formulated, go beyond the scope of direct objects. More specifically, (96) predicts that, since Y can stand for any postverbal constituent, not only direct objects, but all postverbal constituents are subject to the same linear constraint, i. e., no postverbal constituents are cleftable. This is borne out by examples like (97), which would all be grammatical without the CFM *shi*... (*de*):

(97) a. *Zhang San zhao le ni *shi* *liang* *ci* de.
Zhang San seek PERF 2s CFM two time MM
"It is twice that Zhang San has looked for you."
*张三找了你是两次的。

b. *ta huai de *shi* *hen*.
3s bad RESULT. CFM very
"He's indeed very bad."
*他坏得是很。

c. *ta re de *shi* *han* *dou* *liu* *le* *chulai*.
3s hot RESULT. CFM sweat all flow PERF come = out
"He was so hot that he was sweating."
*他热得是汗都流了出来。

(97a) has a postverbal quantifier phrase, (97b) has a postverbal adverb, and (97c) has a postverbal clause. Like direct objects, all such postverbal constituents are uncleftable. Also like direct objects, they can undergo other syntactic processes, resulting in grammatical sentences. For example, the quantifier phrase in (97a), *liang ci*, can be fronted (98a), relativized (98b), questioned (98c), and pseudo-clefted (98d).

(98) a. ta **liang ci** zhao ni ni dou bu zai.
3s two time seek 2s 2s all not in
"Twice when he looked for you, you were not in."
他两次找你你都不在。

b. wo shengbing de na **liang ci**...
1s be = sick MM that two time
"The two times when I was sick..."
我生病的那两次……

c. ta zhao le ni **ji ci**?
3s seek PERF 2s how = many time
"How many times did he look for you?"
他找了你几次?

d. ta zhao ni de cishu shi **liang ci** (, bu shi yi ci).
3s seek 2s MM time = number be two time not be one time
"The number of times he looked for you is twice, (not just once)."
他找你的次数是两次(不是一次)。

Therefore, (96) accounts not only for uncleftability of DO, but also for that of all postverbal constituents.

There are several pieces of evidence in support of this analysis, the first of which involves preposed direct objects. Recall (95a), which has a preposed topicalized object. Chinese has another means of preposing postverbal direct objects with definite reference: the *ba*-construction, whereby an underlying direct object occurs preverbally and is immediately preceded by a preposition-like object marker, *ba*. In both preverbal positions, the direct object becomes cleftable or at least much more so, as in (99):

(99) a. Zhang San *shi ba xin* cong guowai ji lai le.
Zhang San CFM OM letter from abroad mail DIR PERF
"It is the letter that Zhang San mailed from abroad."
张三是把信从国外寄来了。

b. ? *shi xin* Zhang San cong guowai ji lai le.
CFM letter Zhang San from abroad mail DIR PERF
"It is the letter that Zhang San mailed from abroad."
*是信张三从国外寄来了。

In (99a), a preposed object in the *ba*-construction is fully cleftable. For (99b), given appropriate stress and a pause after the cleft focus, the sentence is much more acceptable than (93e), which has a postverbal focus. Therefore, both support (96).

The second kind of evidence relates to indirect objects headed by *gei* "to/ for" and oblique objects headed by *zai* "at" and *dao* "to". Such phrases in Chinese can occur either preverbally or postverbally, with slight semantic difference sometimes. When such a phrase occurs preverbally, it is cleftable, as in (93c), reproduced here as (100a); however, when it occurs postverbally, it is not cleftable, as in (100b):

(100) a. Zhang San cong guowai *shi gei ta* ji xin de.
Zhang San from abroad CFM to 3S mail letter MM
"It is to him that Zhang San mailed the letter from abroad."
张三从国外是给他寄信的。

b. * Zhang San cong guowai ji *shi* *gei* *ta* xin de.
Zhang San from abroad mail CFM to 3S letter MM
"It is to him that Zhang San mailed the letter from abroad."
* 张三从国外寄是给他信的。

Cleftability in such cases depends entirely on whether the focused constituent is preverbal or postverbal, as predicted by (96).

The third piece of evidence comes from an infrequent variation of cleft sentences, as in (101), wherein the direct object is cleftable but must be heavily stressed:

(101) Zhang San cong guowai *shi* ji le yi feng ***xin***.
Zhang San from abroad CFM mail PERF a M letter
"It's a letter that Zhang San mailed from abroad."
张三从国外是寄了一封信。

Theoretically, DO clefting brings (92) and (96) into conflict with each other, in that while (96) prohibits a postverbal CFM, the immediate precedence requirement of (92) for clefting necessitates a postverbal CFM for DO clefting. This conflict is resolved by letting (96) override (92): while (101) respects the word order constraint (96) in that the CFM occurs before the main verb, it seems to violate (92) insofar as the cleft focus is not adjacent to the CFM. This apparent violation, however, is prosodically compensated for by the heavy stress on the focused DO.

What (101) shows, again, is that DO uncleftability is due not to the object itself, but to the word order constraint specified in (96), in the sense that as long as the CFM *shi* occurs before the main verb and (96) is respected, the sentence is grammatical even if the focus may be discontinuous from the CFM.

Finally, as mentioned earlier, all postverbal constituents are uncleftable, which fact would not be captured by any account taking into consideration the CH or DO alone, but is most elegantly accounted for by (96). The word order constraint, therefore, gives a much more plausible account in that uncleftability follows automatically from a more general, already existing constraint in the language. All cases of uncleftability are accounted for without the need for any *ad hoc* explanation.

One may think of sentences like the following as possible counter-examples to (96):

(102) Zhang San cong guowai ji de *shi* yi feng xin.
Zhang San from abroad mail NOM CPL a M letter
"What Zhang San mailed from abroad is a letter."
张三从国外寄的是一封信。

In (102), *shi* occurs after the main verb, yet the sentence is still grammatical. However, as indicated by the glossing and translation, this construction is in fact not a cleft, but a pseudo-cleft construction, where *shi* is used as an equative copula verb, i. e. a main verb, rather than an optional CFM. The difference is that, with *shi* as a main verb, the sentence would require its obligatory presence and would be ungrammatical without it, whereas with *shi* as a CFM, the sentence would still be grammatical as a non-cleft without it. This is seen in (103) (cf. (102)), where *shi* is deleted, resulting in a (verbless) non-sentence, possibly rendered "a letter that Zhang San mailed from abroad":

(103) * Zhang San cong guowai ji de yi feng xin.
张三从国外寄的一封信。

Additional evidence is seen in the ocuse of the nominalizer *de* (Ross 1983) in sentences like (103), which nominalizes the clause before it as a subject NP, the whole sequence before *de* being a headless relative clause. This being the case, the only main verb candidate in the remaining part of the sentence can be none other than *shi*.

Another kind of apparent counterexample is one like (104), where it seems that *shi* occurs after the main verb *kanjian* "see", an apparent violation of (96), yet the sentence is still grammatical:

(104) wo kanjian ta *shi* *zai* *ji* *tian* *yiqian.*
1s see 3S CFM at a = few day ago
"? It is a few days ago that I saw him."
我看见他是在几天以前。

A more plausible analysis of (104), however, would be in terms of topic-comment structure and treat *shi* as the main verb of the sentence. It is argued that the part before *shi* in (104), *wo kanjian ta* "I see him", is a topical clause which represents known information, and the part that follows *shi*, the comment which represents new information, with *shi* as the equative main verb. The whole sentence should have been more accurately translated as "That I saw him was several days ago." Since the alternative analysis as suggested by the translation in (104) would have *wo* "I" as the subject-topic and *kanjian* "see" as the main verb, it is essential to find out whether the subject-topic is *wo* "I" or *wo kanjian ta* "I see him." Arguments for the latter against the former follow.

According to Li & Thompson (1981), two formal devices can be used to distinguish a topic in Chinese: sentence-initial position, and the optional occurrence of pause or pause particles. In Chinese, a topic usually occurs in sentence-initial position, and can be optionally separated from the comment "by a pause or by one of the pause particles [a, ya, me, ne, or ba]" (p. 86). With respect to (104), the first criterion is not very helpful since both *wo* "I" and *wo kanjian ta* "I see him" are sentence-initial. Applying the second criterion, we get (105):

(105) a. wo kanjian ta **ma**, shi zai ji tian yiqian.
1s see 3s PRT CPL at a = few day ago
"As for my seeing him, it was several days ago."
我看见他嘛,是在几天以前。

b. ? wo **ma**, kanjian ta shi zai ji tian yiqian.
1s PRT see 3s CPL at a = few day ago
"As for me, (I) saw him several days ago."
? 我嘛,看见他是在几天以前。

While the topical status of *wo kanjian ta* in (105a) is clear by virtue of its sounding perfectly natural, the problematic (105b) suggests the dubiousness of *wo* "I" as a subject-topic. The implausibility of a pause particle between *wo* "I" and *kanjian ta* "see him" suggests their integrity as an inseparable whole, *viz.* the topic.

Morphologically, one of the topical features is that the verb in a clausal topic tends to show reduced verbness by virtue of being rendered aspectless or tenseless (Givón 1984). This is exactly what is found in (106), where the ungrammaticality is due to presence of the perfective aspect marker, *le*, without which the sentence would be grammatical:

(106) *wo kanjian ta le shi zai ji tian yiqian.
1s see 3s PERF CPL at a = few day ago
"(As for) my seeing him, it was several days ago."
*我看见他了是在几天以前。

If *kanjian* "see" were the main verb, it would not only allow for, but require, a perfective marker in this context. The impossibility of the perfective *le* in (106), then, further suggests that what precedes *shi* in (104) is a topic with reduced verbness.

Finally, given that the absence of *shi* as a CFM will not affect grammaticality of the sentence as a non-cleft whereas the absence of *shi* as a main verb will, if *shi* were analyzed as the CFM in (104), the sentence would still be grammatical as a non-cleft without it, even if the pragmatic meaning had somewhat changed. But this is not the case; to wit

(107) *wo kanjian ta zai ji tian yiqian.
1s see 3s at a = few day ago
"I saw him several days ago."
*我看见他在几天以前。

This is because the temporal phrase as a rule should occur not after, but before, a non-copula verb in Chinese as part of its typological canonical structure. In other words, for the sentence to be grammatical, *shi* has to occur as a copula verb, which can then take a temporal phrase as its complement.

In sum, sentences like (102) and (104) are in fact not counterevidence to the structural constraint (96).

3.2.3 Is *shi* an adverb?

So far, all the evidence has suggested that DO uncleftability in Chinese is caused not by any *ad hoc* constraint with respect to the object *per se*, but by a constraint with respect to the linear order between the Contrastive Focus Marker (CFM) and the main verb. Consequently, the problem of DO uncleftability in

Chinese has no bearing on the proposed Cleftability Hierarchy; rather, it stems from a more general, and possibly typologically conditioned, word order constraint in Chinese which overrides the effect of the CH. However, this linear constraint has so far appeared *ad hoc* in itself, in that it only refers to the order between the CFM and the main verb, and is motivated by DO uncleftability only. The account would be more elegant if it can be shown that (96) is part of an independently motivated constraint and that the solution of the problem follows automatically from something already existing in the language without recourse to any *ad hoc* constraint.

One possibility, as suggested in Huang (1982a), is to treat the CFM *shi* as an adverb which, like most other adverbs, occurs before the main verb. However, there are some problems with this analysis, according to the criterion that, syntactically, members of a class are expected to behave similarly and are in general mutually exclusive. More specifically, the CFM *shi* shows some important syntactic differences from preverbal adverbs such as *jiu* 就 "just", *zhen* 真 "really" and *zhi* 只 "only". First, while no adverb of the kind represented by *jiu*, *zhen* and *zhi* can occur in the A-not-A construction (as in (108a), a typical verbal feature, the CFM *shi* can, as in (108b):

(108) a. *ta *zhen* *bu* *zhen* lai?
3s really not really come
"Is he really coming or not?"
*他真不真来?

b. ta *shi* *bu* *shi* gei Zhang San ji de xin?
3s CFM not CFM to Zhang San mail MM letter
"Is it to Zhang San that he mailed a letter?"
他是不是给张三寄的信?

Clearly, the CFM *shi* behaves differently from the adverbs with respect to this verbal feature.

A similar difference is seen in their respective ability to occur independently as a short answer to yes/no questions. The CFM *shi*, like full verbs in Chinese, can stand alone as a short answer to yes/no questions, whereas the adverbs can not. Compare

(109) a. A: ni lai ma?
2s come Q
"Are you coming?"
你来吗?

B: lai.
come
"Yes."
来。

b. A: ta *shi* *gei Zhang San* ji de xin ma?
3s CFM to Zhang San mail MM letter Q
"Is it to Zhang San that he mailed a letter?"
他是给张三寄的信吗?

B: shi.
CFM
"Yes."
是。

c. A: ni zhen lai ma?
2s really come Q
"Are you really coming?"
你真来吗?

B: *zhen.
really
"Yes."
*真。

The form of the short answer is a full verb in (109a), a CFM in (109b), and an adverb in the ungrammatical (109c). Thus the CFM *shi*, again, behaves differently from adverbs by virtue of showing a higher degree of verbness than the latter. Given such important syntactic differences, it is not very plausible if we treat *shi* as an adverb.

Another argument against treating *shi* as an adverb is that while the adverbs are mutually exclusive among themselves, they can nevertheless cooccur with *shi*, as in (110):

(110) a. *ta *zhen* *jiu* lai.
3s really just come
"Is he really just coming?"
*他真就来。

b. *zheng/jiu* *shi* *ta* *gei* Zhang San ji de xin.
right just CFM 3S to Zhang San mail MM letter

"It is (none other than) he who mailed a letter to Zhang San."

正是/就是他给张三寄的信。

Since one of the important criteria for establishing membership of a morpho-syntactic class is mutual exclusiveness, or complementarity, the fact that *shi* cooccurs with this subclass of adverbs suggests that the former cannot be a possible member of the latter. Therefore, evidence in terms of both the nature of *shi* and syntactic mutual exclusiveness indicates that the analysis of *shi* as an adverb is untenable.

3.2.4 Quasi-verbs and the constraint revisited

If the CFM *shi* is not an adverb, then what is it? To answer this question, I will propose that the CFM *shi* belongs to a class of "quasi-verbs" whose distribution is restricted to the preverbal position, on the basis of syntactic complementarity and the fact that they share many verbal and non-verbal features. These quasi-verbs include modal auxiliary verbs, co-verbs as well as the CFM *shi*. Modal auxiliary verbs in Chinese include words like *neng* 能 "can", *ken* 肯 "will", *keyi* 可以 "may", and *ying*(*gai*)应(该) "should", whose preverbal distribution is exemplified in (111a), with (111b) illustrating that they cannot occur postverbally.

(111) a. ta neng lai.

3s can come

"He can come."

他能来。

b. * ta lai neng.

* 他来能。

Syntactically, modal auxiliary verbs and the CFM are mutually exclusive, as in (112):

(112) a. * wo *neng* *shi* zai jieshang kanjian ta de.

1s can CFM on street see 3s MM

"It's on the street that I could see him."

* 我能是在街上看见他的。

b. * wo *shi* *neng* zai jieshang kanjian ta de.

1s CFM can on street see 3s MM

* 我是能在街上看见她的。

Co-verbs are preposition-like morphemes in Chinese that derive diachronically from verbs but have lost their full verb status (Chao 1968; Li & Thompson 1975,

1981), for example, *cong* 从 "from", *chao* 朝 "toward", *zai* 在 "at", and *gen* 跟 "with". The preverbal distribution of coverbs is exemplified in (113):

(113) a. ta cong Meiguo lai.
3s from America come
"He's from the U. S."
他从美国来。

b. * ta lai cong Meiguo.
* 他来从美国。

The category co-verb, as observed in Li & Thompson (1981), shows some internal variation among its members with regard to cooccurrence with an aspect marker, as a result of different rate of deverbalization among co-verbs. For example, there are some co-verbs which contain *le* or *zhe*, for example *weile* "for (the sake of)" and *yanzhe* "along". Synchronically, however, their cooccurrence with apparent aspect markers should be nullified for the following reason. Morphologically, the occurrence of apparent aspect markers in these co-verbs is non-productive, i. e., these co-verbs are simply "frozen" morphemes which are perceived by the language learner as unanalyzable and must be individually learned by rote. Moreover, such aspect markers are semantically depleted; for example, there is no perfective meaning whatsoever in the coverb *weile* "for (the sake of)". Therefore, it is more appropriate to treat such co-verbs as synchronically incompatible to aspect markers.

The classification of modal verbs, co-verbs and the CFM as "quasi-verbs" is also based on a number of shared verbal and non-verbal features. Firstly, a verb, or sometimes the first syllable of a verb, can occur on both sides of the negative morpheme in the A-not-A structure (Huang 1988), which functions as a sort of *yes/no* question in Chinese. This is seen in (114a), as is also the case with modal verbs (114b), co-verbs (114c), and the CFM (114d), respectively.

(114) a. A: ni *ding* *bu* *ding* piao?
2S reserve not reserve ticket
"Will you reserve a ticket?"
你订不订票?

B: *bu* *ding*.
not reserve
"No."
不订。

b. A: ni *neng* *bu* *neng* wei wo ding piao?
2s can not can for 1s reserve ticket
"Can you reserve a ticket for me?"
你能不能为我订票?

B: *bu* *neng*.
not can
"No."
不能。

c. A: ni *gen* *bu* *gen* wo zou?
2s with not with 1s go
"Are you going with me?"
你跟不跟我走?

B: *bu* *gen*.
not with
"No."
不跟。

d. A: ni *shi* *bu* *shi* wei wo ding de piao?
2s CFM bu CFM for 1s reserve MM ticket
"Is it for me that you reserved the ticket?"
你是不是为我订的票?

B: *bu* *shi*.
not CFM
"No."
不是。

B's responses in (114) also show two other verbal features shared by modal verbs, co-verbs and the CFM, *viz.* that they can be used as a short answer to yes/no questions, a functional equivalent to *yes* in English, and that they can be negated by the negator *bu* 不.

Moreover, like full verbs, the quasi-verbs can cooccur with a delimiting or emphasizing adverbs such as *zhi* 只 "only", *zhen* 真 "really" and *jiu* 就 "just", as in (115), where (115a) shows use of *zhi* 只 or *zhen* 真 before the co-verb *wei* 为 "for"①,

---

① Given that modal auxiliaries, co-verbs and the CFM are subcategories of quasi-verbs, their possible cooccurrence in sentences like (115b) and (115c) does not pose a threat to their quasi-verb status.

(115b) shows their cooccurrence with a modal verb, and (115c), with the CFM:

(115) a. ta *zhi/zhen* wei wo *ding* le piao.
3s only really for 1s reserve PERF ticket
"He only/really reserved a ticket for me."
他只/真为我订了票。

b. ta *zhi/zhen* *neng* wei wo ding piao.
3s only really can for 1s reserve ticket
"He can only/really reserve a ticket for me."
他只/真能为我订票。

c. ta *zhi/zhen* *shi* wei wo ding de piao.
3s only really CFM for 1s reserve MM ticket
"It is only/really for me that he reserved a ticket."
他只/真是为我订的票。

Apart from the above verbal features shared by modal auxiliaries, co-verbs and the CFM, there are also several non-verbal features shared by them. First of all, while a full verb used as the main verb in a sentence can generally take any of the aspectual morphemes such as the perfective-*le*, the progressive-*zhe*, and the experiential-*guo*, as exemplified in (115a), no aspectual morpheme can be used with a modal auxiliary ((116a)), a co-verb ((116b)), or the CFM ((116c)):

(116) a. * ta zuotian *neng-le* wei ni ding piao.
3s yesterday can-PERF for 2s reserve ticket
"He could reserve a ticket for you yesterday."
* 他昨天能了为你订票。

b. * ta *cong-le* guowai ding piao.
3s from-PERF broad reserve ticket
"He booked the ticket from abroad."
* 他从了国外订票。

c. * ta *shi-le* wei ni ding de piao.
3s CFM-PERF for 2s reserve MM ticket
"It was for you that he reserved a ticket."
* 他是了为你订的票。

Also, a full verb is morphologically reduplicable in full or in part for various purposes, whereas modal auxiliaries, co-verbs or the CFM are not. For example, a volitional verb may be reduplicated to mark a diminutive aspect (See Li & Thompson

1981: 232-36 for details), as in (117a), but this reduplication is not possible with modal auxiliaries (117b), co-verbs (117c) or the CFM (117d), respectively.

(117) a. ni *kankan* zhe ben shu.
2s look-look this M book
"You read this book (for a while)."
你看看这本书。

b. * ta *nengneng* kan zhe ben shu.
3s can-can look this M book
"He can read this book."
* 他能能看这本书。

c. * ta congcong tushuguan jie shu
3s from-from library borrow book
"He borrows books from the library."
* 他从从图书馆借书。

d. * *shishi* ta kan zhe ben shu de.
CFM-CFM 3s look this M book MM
"It is he who read this book."
* 是是他看这本书的。

Finally, while the verb is usually an indispensable constituent in a grammatical sentence①, a modal auxiliary, co-verb② or the CFM is dispensable in that its absence would generally not affect grammaticality, although the resulting sentence may to some extent differ semantically from the original one. This omissibility of quasi-verbs is shown in (118):

(118) a. tamen (hui) tan gangqin.
3PL can play piano
"They (can) play the piano."
他们(会)弹钢琴。

b. tamen (zai xuexiao) tan gangqin.

---

① Like many other languages, verbless sentences exist in Chinese, especially in the colloquial variety. However, since what is concerned with here is whether *in general* a sentence should require the presence of a verb, we will not consider possible verbless sentences in the language.

② When a co-verb is omitted, it takes with it its complement.

3s at school play piano
"They play the piano (at the school)."
他们(在学校)弹钢琴。

c. (shi) tamen zai tan gangqin.
CFM 3PL PROG play piano
"(It is) they (who) are playing the piano."
(是)他们在弹钢琴。

Despite the fact that the CFM can occur pre-nominally whereas modal auxiliaries and co-verbs can not, we have seen that they share a number of verbal and non-verbal features. Table 3.2 summarizes these shared features. Since all the categories show positive values for some of the parameters but negative values for the others, the term "quasi-verb" serves to unify the categories. Table 3.2, then, provides a valid basis for classifying modal verbs, co-verbs and the CFM *shi* as subcategories of "quasi-verbs", which all occur preverbally.

Table 3.2 ***Shared verbal and non-verbal features of modal auxiliaries and the Contrastive Focus Marker in Chinese***

Feature	Verb	Quasi-Verb		
		Modal	Co-Verb	CFM
1. A-not-A	+	+	+	+
2. Short Answer	+	+	+	+
3. Negation	+	+	+	+
4. Cooccurrence with adverb	+	+	+	+
5. Cooccurrence with aspect marker	+	–	–	–
6. Reduplication	+	–	–	–
7. Obligatory occurrence	–	–	– ①	–

Given these quasi-verbs, we are now able to generalize the linear constraint (96) as (118), which states that a quasi-verb must not occur after the main verb in

① Due to their slower rate of deverbalization, some co-verbs, such as *gei* 给 "to", *zai* 在 "at" and *dao* 到 "toward", can still be used as full verbs, and when so used, they are obligatory.

a sentence.

(119) *X MV QV Y

(119) exists independently as a word order constraint between a quasi-verb and the main verb in Chinese. Since it rules out the possibility of a quasi-verb occurring postverbally, DO uncleftability is automatically accounted for, and no other *ad hoc* explanation is needed.

3.2.5 Summary

To sum up, DO uncleftability in Chinese as apparent counterevidence to the Cleftability Hierarchy has been shown to be due not to the inherent property of direct objects or inapplicability of the CH itself, but to a constraint on the linear structure which is in conflict with, and overrides the effect of, the CH. Since the constraint, which crucially involves the order of a quasi-verb and the main verb in Chinese, is independently motivated in the language, no *ad hoc* account is needed to account for DO uncleftability in Chinese. Thus it is seen that while the CH attains some measure of plausibility as a language universal, it nevertheless can interact with, and be negatively affected by, language specific constraints.

3.3 Conclusion

In Chapter 2 and this chapter, we have initially developed some criteria according to which we can measure cleftability of different constituents on the Cleftability Hierarchy. Using these criteria, we then examined crosslinguistic data which support the proposed CH in the following ways:

(i) Clefting of higher positions on the CH is in general more grammatical than that of lower positions in terms of the same clefting strategy, and that promotion to higher positions can facilitate clefting.

(ii) The deletion strategy tends to be used for clefting of higher positions on the CH, and the pronoun retention strategy, a more marked strategy which is supposedly more facilitating to processing, is used for clefting of lower positions.

(iii) Clefting of higher positions occurs in wider distribution or more frequently than clefting of lower positions.

(iv) Diachronic change results in continuous segments of the Cleftability Hierarchy rather than leave a gap on it.

(v) Some apparent counterexamples may be the result of interplay between the CH and other parts of the grammar, such as transitivity, language-specific constraints, or typological features.

In conclusion, crosslinguistic evidence has, in various ways, supported the proposed Cleftability Hierarchy, which in turn conforms to the AH. The AH, therefore, has shown its validity not only with relativization but also with clefting of NP arguments.

As for why the AH works the way it does, e. g. why SU is more accessible than DO, it is held here is that the AH can be viewed as in general reflecting different degrees of structural embeddedness, as can be seen in (120):

(120)
```
          IP
        /    \
    NP1      VP
            /   \
          V'     PP
         /  \     |
        V  NP2   P'
                / \
               P  NP3
```

In (120), NP_1 (subject) is the least embedded and NP_3 (oblique) whose case is head-assigned is the most embedded. The levels of embeddedness with different NP arguments correspond to the ordering on the AH. If we take the position that the level of embeddedness correlates with the degree of structural complexity, then the AH can be said to reflect a scale of structural complexity of different NP arguments, in the sense that structurally less embedded NP arguments are more accessible, whereas structurally more embedded NP arguments are less accessible. Therefore, for example, direct objects are more accessible than oblique objects because they occur in a structurally less embedded position where information is more easily processed.

Finally, although the CH has been shown to be a plausible universal tendency, it should be noted that we have only dealt with NP arguments in our discussion. This is natural considering that the AH from which the CH was derived was developed out of studies on relativization, which can operate only on NPs. Clefting, on the other hand, differs from relativization in that it can operate on non-NPs as well as NPs. Therefore, observational adequacy can not be achieved by resorting to the AH alone.

Moreover, even for the syntactic positions specified by the AH, information other than syntactic can be crucial in determining cleftability. Consider the following examples from English:

(121) a. ? *It is to please John that is easy.

b. *It is that linguistics is fun that he thinks.

The sentences in (121) with a clefted subject, which is supposed to be the most cleftable, turn out to be problematic. The reason for this, as shown in Chapter 4, lies in the nature of the lexical head of the clefted constituent; more specifically, this seems to be related to the degree of nouniness of the lexical head. Moreover, it is generally noted that adjuncts enjoy much higher cleftability than most kinds of NP arguments, as shown in Table 2.9 on intralinguistic frequency of occurrence (2.5.1) and Table 2.10 on crosslinguistic frequency of occurrence (2.5.2). This is probably due to some semantic-pragmatic principle concerning the notion of thematicity. Thus, descriptive adequacy of cleftability relies on at least three kinds of information: syntactic, lexical, and pragmatic. Chapter 4 and Chapter 5 deal with lexical and pragmatical information, respectively.

Chapter 4 Non-NP Cleftability

4.1 Introduction

In Chapter 3, it was concluded that crosslinguistically, cleftability of various NP arguments in general conforms to the proposed Cleftability Hierarchy in various ways, which in turn supports Keenan and Comrie's Accessibility Hierarchy in the context of clefting. What should be borne in mind, however, is that the Accessibility Hierarchy was originally proposed on the basis of studies of relativization, which, despite its many similarities with cleft constructions, differs from clefting both functionally and structurally. Functionally, although clefting and relativization are both devices for foregrounding (Schachter 1973), they have quite different communicative roles. For relativization, its major communicative function is to "provide names for, or ways of designating, the multitude of entities that people wish to talk about, but for which there is no established single-noun designation" (Schachter 1973:43). For clefting, its major function is thematic focusing (Brömser 1984; Declerck 1984; Collins 1987, 1991). Structurally, relativization pertains only to NPs, whereas clefting affects not only NPs but also non-NP constituents such as PPs, sometimes ADVPs, occasionally APs, and rarely VPs in some languages. Consequently, for a grammar to adequately describe and account for cleftability, it must consider non-NP as well as NP cleftability. Therefore, the domain of the Cleftability Hierarchy should be larger than that of the Accessibility Hierarchy.

This larger domain of the Cleftability Hierarchy requires that it be extended in some way to accommodate non-NP constituents. One way to achieve this is by extending the Hierarchy so that it includes non-NPs in certain order at different positions on the Hierarchy. A hypothetical hierarchy of this kind which resembles the idea briefly mentioned in Pinkham and Hankamer (1975) would look like (122):

(122) SU > DO > IO > ... PP > ADVP > AP > VP

There are several difficulties with such an extended hierarchy. Firstly, as attested in many languages, including English (Collins 1987, 1991), PPs tend to have higher cleftability than most types of NPs except subject. Therefore, to put PP toward the lower end of the extended hierarchy would be empirically unsupportable. Secondly, the ranked categories are not consistent: while the left-end categories refer to grammatical functions, the right-end ones are phrasal categories. Such inconsistency makes the comparison of cleftability difficult, if not impossible. Finally, a consequence of such an extended hierarchy is that a certain degree of inherent cleftability has to be assumed of these non-NPs, independent of context.

The alternative is to treat non-NPs as in general having low cleftability, without specifying their exact position on the Cleftability Hierarchy. Their cleftability, however, depends on context and is determined by some general principle. The subsequent representation of this alternative would be a partially unordered segment toward the lower end of the extended Hierarchy, a segment whose non-NP members' cleftability is determined by context and some general principle which both supplements and in part accounts for the Cleftability Hierarchy. As will be seen later, the context-free solution is empirically not plausible, as many apparently uncleftable non-NP constituents often become more cleftable in certain contexts. On the other hand, varying degrees of grammaticality with, for example, clefted APs, VPs and ADVPs in different contexts make it virtually impossible to specify a fixed position for such constituents on the Cleftability Hierarchy. Therefore, the context-sensitive approach will be adopted in which the Cleftability Hierarchy is extended by virtue of some principle referring to prototypes of phrases.

To accommodate the difficulties mentioned above, certain revisions on (122) will have to be made; but for ease of discussion, we will start with the added categories in (122).

The organization of Chapter 3 is as follows: through an initial examination of AP-clefting in English, a Nouniness Principle will be hypothesized, against which AP-clefting, VP-clefting, PP-clefting and ADVP-clefting will then be examined in that order.

4.2 AP Cleftability

4.2.1 The Nouniness Principle

As mentioned earlier, clefting as a syntactic process is widely applicable to NPs and PPs but not to APs and VPs in a great many languages, due to the latters' non-argument status (Emonds 1976). Adjective phrases (APs), due to their non-argument status, are in general uncleftable in many languages. For example, clefting of APs in English results in ungrammaticality in (123):

(123) a. * It is quiet that the e man lost his temper. (Heggie 1988:227)

b. * It is happy that he is e.

c. * It's mellow that Bill [finds] Susan e.

In terms of grammatical function, the clefted AP in (123a) is attributive, that in (123b) is predicative, and the one in (123c) is the predicate of a small clause. In all the cases, the APs are uncleftable. Another category which is treated as AP in this study is predicational NPs of indefinite reference, which are usually felt to be adjectival in nature, even if they take the form of NPs. This is supported by the fact that, like adjectives, such predicational NPs are relativized as *which* rather than *who* in the following kind of non-restrictive clauses with a [+ human] antecedent:

(124) a. This is Mary, who/ * which you have already met.

b. She is clever, which/ * who you are not.

c. She is *a genius*, which/ * who you are not.

In (124c), the relative pronoun of the predicational NP antecedent *a genius* follows an adjectival pattern as that in (124b), rather than a nominal pattern as in (124a). Moreover, such predicational NPs are in general as uncleftable as predicative APs, as in

(125) * It is a genius that she is. (cf. (123b))

Structural properties like these, then, justify treating such predicational NPs as APs.

However, in certain discourse contexts and structural configurations, APs can become more cleftable (Declerck 193, 1984b; Quirk et al. 1985; Pinkham & Hankamer 1975; Lumsden & Lefbvre 1990). One kind of apparent counterexamples to the claim that APs of the above kinds are uncleftable, as has been noted in Quirk et al. (1985), Heggie (1988), and Pinkham and Hankamer (1975), are colour adjectives used in sentences like the following:

(126) It's **dark green** that we've painted the kitchen e. (Quirk et al. 1985)

Several possible explanations are discussed in Heggie (1988) with regard to cleftability of colour adjectives as shown in (126). The first one simply treats colour adjectives as an *ad hoc* class of adjectives which are somehow susceptible to clefting. However, it falls apart if only one considers sentences like (127), which show that colour adjectives are as uncleftable as other adjectives:

(127) a. * It's blue that the barn could be. (Heggie 1988:228)

b. * It's white that I saw John turn.

The second possible explanation takes into account the semantic aspect of the clefted colour adjective and attributes its cleftability to its resultative interpretation in sentences like (126). This is again quickly dismissed by examples like (128), which show that resultative APs are in general uncleftable:

(128) a. * It's tough that Bill cooked the meal. (Heggie 1988:228)

b. * It's flat that they hammer the nail.

A third explanation, suggested by Heggie (1988), analyzes the clefted AP in (126) as an optional argument of the verb *to paint*, i. e. the colour term is in fact nominal rather than adjectival. Evidence in support of this analysis includes first of all semantic relatedness between the verb and the colour term. More specifically, while a colour is implied with a verb like *to paint*, "there is no similar implication of 'toughness' with the verb *to cook* or of 'flatness' with the verb *to hammer*" (Heggie 1988: 229). Moreover, a comparison between the interrogative WH-words used in WH-questions based on (126) and (128b) reveals some crucial difference in support of the nominal analysis of colour terms: while *what*, a typical argument operator, is used to replace the colour term in (129a), *how*, an adjunct operator, is used in place of the adjective in (129b) of a similar structure:

(129) a. A: What/ * How did they paint the house?

B: Dark green.

b. A: How/ * What did they hammer the nail?

B: Flat.

Thus the colour term in (126) behaves like a NP argument and, as such, is cleftable like other NPs.

Heggie's analysis of the clefted colour term not only accounts for the morphological difference revealed in (129) as well as cleftability of colour adjectives, it is also suggestive of a more general principle regarding cleftability, *viz*. the nominal properties of cleftable elements, especially cleftable non-NP constituents. Despite its plausibility, Heggie's analysis, as will be shown, fails to capture neither the distinct adjectival features of colour terms nor those colour terms that are morphologically marked with overt adjectival affixes. It is therefore contended that examples like (126) should be more appropriately analyzed as an adjective having acquired some nominal features and become more noun-like. The argument proceeds as follows. Consider the following example:

(130) It's greenish that they painted the house.

Unlike (126), in which the colour term is morphologically unmarked and can be interpreted as either adjectival or nominal, in (130), the adjectivizing suffix-*ish* unequivocally marks *greenish* as an adjective, which, like the clefted colour term in (126), can be questioned with *what* rather than *how*:

(131) A: What/ * How did they paint the house?

B: Greenish.

Given that *greenish* can only be adjectival, Heggie's explanation would not be applicable here to account for grammaticality of (130). On the other hand, *greenish* and other colour terms do show the nominal property of being substitutable by *what* but not *how* in Wh-questions. The question remains whether there is a more principled and plausible way of accounting for cleftability of colour terms in particular and AP cleftability in general.

The answer seems to lie in a nominality analysis from a prototypical perspective, which differs from Heggie's nominal analysis by examining the extent to which colour terms and other APs exhibit nominal features rather than treating them as inherently and categorically nominal; and it is this increased degree of nominality, together with semantic relatedness noted in Heggie (1988), that makes colour terms more cleftable. Therefore, treating colour terms not as inherently nominal but as adjectives with certain degree of nominality enables us to account for both increased cleftability of colour terms in given contexts and their inherent adjectival features such as gradability.

As suggested above, the nominal properties of colour terms in relation to their cleftability may be generalizable to a principle regarding cleftability, especially that of non-NP constituents. On the basis of the nominality analysis, and following Pinkham and Hankamer (1975), a "Nouniness Principle" will be proposed here to account for cleftability of non-NP constituents in general that also subsumes NP cleftability:

(132) **The Nouniness Principle**

The more noun-like a constituent is, the more cleftable it tends to be.

where being more noun-like is defined both structurally and semantico-pragmatically. Structurally, a non-NP is more noun-like if it shows morphological and/or syntactic markings that are usually associated with NPs, such as the -ing gerundive verb marking in English and argument position for the clefted non-NP in the underlying structure. Pragmatically, a non-NP is more noun-like if it exhibits semantico-pragmatic features typically associated with NPs, such as specificity and definiteness. In the following discussion on cleftability of APs and other kinds of phrases, we will examine crosslinguistic evidence regarding the Nouniness Principle.

4.2.2 Cleftability of predicational APs: the Specificity Condition

The subtitle of this section reflects a concern raised in 3.3, that cleftability of sentence constituents should rely on information of both phrasal category and grammatical function. Linguists who have considered both phrasal categorial information and grammatical functional information are usually of the opinion that a cleft whose focal item functions as an underlying post-copula predicative in the presupposed clause is often unacceptable, or at least questionable:

(133) a. * It is a genius that he is. (Leech & Svartvik 1975:181)

b. * It is the football coach that John is. (Emonds 1976:140)

Based on such observations, Emonds (1976: 140) makes the assertion that "predicative nominatives and predicate adjectives do not appear in focus position in the cleft construction." Lee (1963: 380) had expressed a similar view. However, as will be shown, this asserted restriction on cleftability of predicative elements can be reversed or relaxed depending on context and according to a semantico-pragmatic condition which conforms to (132).

In Akmajian (1979) and Higgins (1976), copula sentences are classified into "specificational" and "predicational". A copular sentence is specificational if one of the NPs (usually the subject NP) represents a variable for which the other NP (usually the predicative NP) specifies a value:

(134) A: Who's the chairman of the committee?

B: The chairman is John Smith.

In (134), the NP representing the variable (i.e. *chairman*) normally resembles the heading of a list, the value of which is specified by the predicative definite NP *John Smith*. On the other hand, a copular sentence is predicational if the predicative NP/AP does not represent a value specified for a variable but functions as a sort of semantic predicate, in the sense that it does not identify the referent of the subject NP but simply provides more information about it. Usually, the predicational NP in this case describes a property or a role, or indicates class membership:

(135) a. Mary is a pretty girl/a teacher.

b. He is a Canadian.

In (135a), *a pretty girl* describes a property of the subject NP, *Mary*; or *a teacher* states a role of *Mary*. In (135b), the predicational NP describes the class membership (i. e. Canadian) of the subject NP. Unlike the subject NP in a specificational sentence which represents a variable, the subject NP in a predicational sentence is already quite definite. Functionally, the post-copula constituent is identificational in a specificational sentence but descriptive in a predicational one. Structurally, while the pre-copular and post-copular NPs in specificational sentences are reversible, those in predicational sentences are not, as can be seen in the ungrammatical **A teacher is Mary*.

The cleft sentence is essentially a specificational type of sentence, in that the cleft focus is almost always identificational and the presupposed part always represents a variable. An important feature required of the value assigned to a variable is that it needs to be specific by virtue of having some exclusive meaning. It is this specificity (and related exclusiveness) that affects cleftability of predicative elements in predicational sentences. As attested earlier, such predicative element, even if they may take the form of an NP, are usually felt to be adjectival, and as such are not felt to be exclusive in meaning, because one characteristic does not automatically exclude other characteristics someone or something may have. For example, as Declerck (1984) augues, to say *Mary is pretty* does not exclude diligence as another characteristic that Mary may have. If we relate such lack of exclusiveness to low specificity, we may say that a predicational constitient is generally uncleftable because it fails to meet the specificity requirement of a cleftable constituent.

Where we do find cleft sentences with a predicational constitient as the cleft focus, we also tend to find increased exclusiveness, and subsequently increased specificity, in the predicational element, as in

(136) A: What is Mary's most typical characteristic? (Declerck 1984:135)

B: It is pretty that Mary is e, more than anything else.

(137) a. * It is a good citizen that he is not.

b. If there is one thing that he is not, it is a good citizen.

The increased exclusiveness in the predicational constituents in (136) and (137) is generated by the context. In (136), the answer in the context of the preceding question implies that being pretty and not any other characteristic is most typical of Mary. Similarly, while (137a) is unacceptable if used in isolation, (137b) is much better because the nominalness (i. e. *the thing that he is not*) and exclusiveness is created by the context. Therefore, for a predicational constituent to be the cleft focus, it needs to be specific in the context. This can be more formally stated as the Specificity Condition in (138):

(138) **the Specificity Condition**

A predicational element is not cleftable unless it is made more specific by the context.

4.2.3 Contextually generated specificity: English

One way specificity is structurally coded is through use of modifiers such as various kinds of adjuncts, which specifies the scope within which the proposition is true. Generally, modified predicational elements are more specific, and more cleftable, than bare predicational elements. To wit,

(139) a. * It is happy that he is e.

b. ? It is happy that he always is e whenever I see him.

(140) a. * It was willing that he appeared e.

b. It is willing that he must appear e, if he is to succeed in this interview.

The sentences in (139) and (140) differ in three ways: (i) degree of grammaticality, with (140b) being more acceptable than (139b), and (139a) and (140a) being simply unacceptable; (ii) whether the predication is modified by some adjunct, and (iii) whether the link verb is *be*. We note that while (139a) and (140a) have unmodified predicates, (139b) and (140b) both have adjuncts which help create a rather specific setting for the predicates. On the other hand, whereas (139a-b) use the copula *be*, (140a-b) use the non-*be* link verb *appear*. Semantically, non-*be* link verbs are less depleted, i. e. more substantial, than the copula *be*, and therefore more specific. As Declerck (1984: 145) points out, unlike *be*, link verbs like *look*, *become*, *appear*, *grow*, etc. " express a predicational relation that is more readily linked up with specific circumstances or with a specific time." The property assigned to the referent of the subject NP is therefore more easily felt to be exclusive: it is the particular property that the referent has or had in specific circumstances. Therefore, both presence of adjuncts and the use of a non-*be* link verb increase specificity for the clefted AP in (140b), making it the most cleftable of the four sentences.

Another way to show increased specificity of a clefted predicational constituent, as implied in the discussion so far, is to see whether it has a strong contrastive reading from the context. Contextually, it is possible to identify cleft sentences as having a weak contrastive reading or a strong contrastive reading, as illustrated in (141):

(141) a. A: Who hit John? (Heggie 1988:205)

B: It's Mary who e hit John.

b. A: Who hit John?

B: Mary did.

C: No, it's Bill (not Mary) who e hit John.

The difference between (141a) and (141b) is that while (141a) only gets a weak contrastive reading, (141b) is a strong contrastive statement to a prior utterance. Despite this difference, both (141a) and (141b) are grammatical.

The significance of the contrast between weak and strong contrastive reading is more clearly seen in clefted predicational APs, as shown in (142).

(142) a. A: What colour are her eyes? (Heggie 1988: 206)

B: * It's green that her eyes are.

b. A: What colour are her eyes?

B: Her eyes are green.

C: No, it's BLUE that her eyes are, not GREEN.

(142) parallels (141) in that contextually, (142a) gets a weak contrastive reading whereas (142b) a strong contrastive reading. It differs from (141) in that while the degree of contrastiveness does not affect grammaticality of (141), where NPs are clefted, it does negatively affect cleftability of predicational APs with a weak contrastive reading, as shown in (142a). More importantly, as (141) and (142) show, predicational APs tend to become more cleftable when made more contrastively specific by the context. Also, NPs are more cleftable than APs by virtue of wider distribution (i. e. in clefts with strong or weak contrastive reading). In other words,

the less nominal constituent is syntactically more constrained with regard to clefting. As another example of greater cleftability being reflected in wider distribution, consider (143):

(143) a. Susan said that it was John that Mary hit e and Jane said it was Tom.

b. * Susan said that it's stupid that John is e and Mary said that it's clever.

Both (143a) and (143b) have coordinate clauses embedded in the matrix sentence, with the VP deleted from the second of the conjoined clauses under identity. However, while an NP can be clefted from such an embedded clause, as in (143a), a predicational AP cannot, as in (143b). Given the criterion set forth in (17c) of Chapter 2, that greater cleftability is reflected in wider distribution, what is obvious here is that cross-categorially, NP arguments are more cleftable than APs.

A comparison between (142b) and (143b) reveals further that the Specificity Condition alone may not fully account for cleftability of predicational APs; we have to consider syntactic complexity such as embedding, such that the more deeply embedded a constituent, the less cleftable it tends to be. More specifically, in (143b) the context yields a strong contrastive reading similar to that in (142b), but since the clefting in (143b) is from embedded clauses whereas that in (142b) is from a matrix sentence, (142b) allows a clefted AP but (143b) does not. This is due not to specificity, but to syntactic complexity: even if a predicational AP is made more specific by the context, syntactic constraints may still prevent it from being clefted. Therefore, both semantico-pragmatic factors and syntactic factors, and their interaction thereof, should be considered when dealing with AP cleftability.

4.2.4 Summary

Generally speaking, APs are either uncleftable or have low cleftability compared with NPs. However, through a nominality analysis, it has been shown that while attributive APs are uncleftable in all cases, predicational APs may become more cleftable if it meets the Specificity Condition under the following circumstances:

(144) a. the predicate has a restrictive modifier, which provides the cleft focus with an exclusive meaning that in turn makes the AP more specific;

b. the cleft focus has a strong, contextually-generated contrastive reading which makes an AP more specific; and/or

c. the clefted AP exhibits nominal properties structurally.

The Specificity Condition is entailed in the Nouniness Principle (132), in that semantically, specificity is a typical nominal feature. This is widely attested in the world's languages in which semantic differences in terms of reference (specific or non-specific) are coded on the nouns by distinct grammatical devices. It has also been shown that the Specificity Condition interacts with distributional possibilities and syntactic complexity, in order to give a fuller account of AP cleftability. It will be seen that the same Nouniness Principle and other structural properties are also responsible for other kinds of non-NPs, to which we will turn next.

4.3 VP Cleftability

4.3.1 Limitations and conditions

It is observed that the syntactic process of clefting is limited in many languages to nominal and some adverbial arguments of the clause only. In these languages, clefting a VP is normally impossible. For example, the following sentences in English are ruled out as ungrammatical:

(145) a. * It was talking that they were. (Bolinger 1972:113)

b. * It is sit that he does.

c. * It's killing that Joe did to the goat. (Givón 1990:731)

The same is presumably true of other languages, for example Berber (146) and Danish (147):

Berber (Ennaji & Sadiqi 1986:60)

(146) a. i-dda hmad

3S-left Ahmed

"Ahmed left."

b. * **i-dda** *a* hmad

3S-left COMP Ahmed

"It's left that Ahmed did."

Danish (NØlke 1984)

(147) ? * Det er grædt, hun har.

it is weeped she has

" * It's weeped that she has."

Two cognitively-based explanations are provided in Givón (1990: 731) to account for such VP uncleftability. Functionally, clefting involves a topicalized stable entity, not a state or event. Therefore, it is generally compatible with NPs but not with VPs and such. Structurally, clefting the verb would leave the remaining portion of the clause without its core, thus hard to interpret. Furthermore, no prototypical relative clause-like structure such as that in the presupposed part of a cleft sentence can be obtained without the verb. Evidence for the functional explanation is found in an iconic mapping between the function of clefts and crosslinguistic structural similarities between clefting and topicalization (Chomsky 1977, Percival 1981, Kimenyi 1978). Evidence for the structural explanation is found in several languages, including English, where VP-clefting is possible in certain structural configurations. In these languages, the VP-clefting construction tends to exhibit one or more salient structural features which help increase the nouniness of the clefted element on the one hand and help maximally preserve the logical structure of the original sentence on the other, hence reducing the processing difficulty. Two such structural features are given in Givón (1990: 732):

(148) a. The cleft-focused verb takes a non-finite, nominal form.

b. In the topic-clause portion of the construction, the verb is repeated in its *finite* form, in its neutral position.

(148a) is similar to a requirement for AP clefting in English discussed in 4.2. Both AP-clefting and VP-clefting reflect the general principle of nouniness, in that once rendered more noun-like through some nominalization process, what is originally an uncleftable non-NP may now be more cleftable in some languages. (148b), on the other hand, is reminiscent of the pronoun retention strategy mentioned in Criterion (17b) for NP cleftability measurement, only that what is being used here is a verb copy rather than a pronominal copy. Functionally, however, both pronoun retention and verb copy serve to preserve the logical structure of the sentence, hence facilitating processing.

In what follows, we will look at crosslinguistic evidence for the structural features mentioned in (148). In addition, it will be shown that these structural accounts again interact with the Specificity Condition, to give a more inclusive account of the data to be examined. However, all these are subsumed under the more general Nouniness Principle.

4.3.2 Crosslinguistic evidence

The languages examined in this section include English, Yoruba, Berber,

Breton, Hausa, Vata, and Haitian creole, each reflecting the above mentioned features in a different way.

4.3.2.1 Morpho-syntactic nominality of clefted VPs: English, Berber, Breton, and Hausa

While the English cleft sentences in (145) are ungrammatical, clefting of verbs seems to be easier when they are the sole constituents of the VP (149b), or when the entire VP rather than the verb alone is clefted (149a, 149c) (Givón 1990:731):

(149) a. ? It's going to the market that he then did. (Givón 1990:731)

b. ? It's working that he did.

c. ?? It's drinking beer from the bottle that she keeps doing.

(Heggie 1988: 226)

Structurally, (149) differ from (145) in two respects. Categorially, the cleft foci are maximal projections of V (i. e. the entire VP) in (149), but V^0 (the head) in (145). This may manifest a universal tendency, *viz.* that clefting is sensitive to the maximal projection of a phrasal category (= XP) only. Morphologically, unlike the participial form in (145a), the focused VPs in (149) take a nominalized form, the gerundial *-ing* ending, although the two forms are homophonous. It follows that the verbal form, *do*, must be analyzed as a pro-verb subcategorizing for a following NP (i. e. DO), similar to that in sentences like *She did some shopping*. According to this analysis, greater cleftability of the VPs in (149) may be attributed to their nominal features, which render the sentences more cleftable. Thus, the Nouniness Principle is supported.

Another language in which we find similar evidence is Berber. We have seen earlier in (146) that a VP with a finite verb head in Berber is not cleftable at all. By contrast, however, VPs with non-finite verb heads can undergo clefting, as in (150):

Berber (Ennaji & Sadiqi 1986:60)

(150)	*a*	*i-ddu*	*a*	t-ra	fadma
	to	he-go	CFM	she-want	Fadma

" * It's for him to go that Fadma wants."

We note that the initial cleft focus marked by the focus marker, *a*, is preceded by another *a*, which is the infinitive marker in Berber. The case resembles that of English discussed above, in that on the one hand, the cleft focus occupies an underlying NP argument position syntactically, which is shown by the verb *ra* "want" that subcategorizes for a direct object; on the other hand, the infinitive marker makes the VP tenseless, a deverbalizing feature that renders the clefted VP less verb-like and more noun-like. Again, we see a case where increased cleftability is correlated with increased nouniness.

A third language that provides evidence for clefted VPs being nominalized is Breton, a VSO language where a constituent is clefted by occurring in initial position followed by the CFM *eo*. VP-clefting is generally impossible, except in sentences like the following:

Breton (Timm 1987:132)

(151) *rentan servij dit eo* a fell din
render service to-you CFM PRT it-want to-me
"It's serving you that I want to do."

(152) *mont d'ar ger diouzhtu eo* a ri
go to-the house immediately CFM PRT 2S-FUT-do
"It's going home immediately that you'll do."

(153) n' *eo* ket *refuzin eo* a ran
NEG CFM NEG refuse CFM PRT 1s-do
"It isn't that I am *refusing*." (lit., "It isn't refuse that I do.")

In (151-153) all the clefted VPs seem to take the original verb form with no apparent nominal morphology. However, as Timm (1987) argues, the clefted VP should be treated as verbal nouns, whose nominal status is seen in the use of *a*, a verbal particle that often appears in a relative clause or a clefting structure if the relativized or clefted constituent functions as subject or direct object in the clause, as contrasted with *e*, the counterpart of *a* in cases where the relativized or clefted constituent is non-subject and non-object (Timm 1987: 135-7). This contrast is shown in (154) and (155), where a clefted subject NP or object NP cooccurs with the particle *a*, and (156), where a clefted PP adjunct cooccurs with the particle *e*:

(154) *te eo* **a** zo kiriek (Timm 1987)
2S CFM PRT CPL responsible
"It's you who is responsible."

(155) n'*eo* ket *se eo* **a** lavaran
NEG-CFM NEG that CFM PRT 1s-say
"It's not that that I'm saying."

(156) *gantho* *c'hoar-gaer* *eo* **e** c'hoantefen kaozeal
with-2PL-GEN sister-beautiful CFM PRT 1s-would-like speak
"... it's with your sister-in-law that I'd like to speak."

The use of *a* in (151-153), then, clearly indicates that although there is no overt morphological marking in its form, the clefted VP is actually a verbal-noun, which functions like a direct object to the verb. As in other cases, this nominal status should be considered responsible for VP cleftability in Breton.

Hausa, a Chadic language with a basic SVO order, is another language which permits some kind of VP-clefting but requires that the clefted VP take nominal morphology. As an example, consider (157):

Hausa (Tuller 1986:428)

(157) *cin* *abincii* *da* *saurii*, aka cee sun / suka yi
eat-VN food with speed INDEF say 3-PERF 3-REL do
"It is eating food in a hurry that someone said they did."

(157) reflects a number of structural properties mentioned earlier. First, the cleft focus includes the verb head (V^0) together with its complement and adjunct, i.e. the clefted constituent is the entire VP. Secondly, the clefted VP, as reflected in the gloss, bears nominal morphology and should be more appropriately analyzed as a verbal noun. This nominal status of the fronted VP enables the VP to be clefted without causing ungrammaticality. Thirdly, the lower verb *yi* "do" is a kind of proverb which helps to preserve the canonical structure of the clause. Thus, like the other languages already discussed, Hausa also provides evidence for the Nouniness Principle.

4.3.2.2 The retention strategy for VP clefting: Vata, Yoruba, and Haitian

As a much less frequent alternative of facilitating processing of cleft sentences with clefted VPs, a few languages have been found to use a strategy analogical to the pronoun retention strategy discussed in terms of (17b) of Chapter 2. In these languages, a verb copy is left in the underlying position from which a finite verb has been clefted. The clefted verb may take nominal morphology but does not necessarily do so. In contrast to VP-clefting examined in 4.3.2.1, what is clefted in these languages is usually a V^0, i.e. a verb head without any complement or adjunct.

Three such languages are reported, Vata and Haitian creole in Lumsden & Lefebvre (1990), and Yoruba in Bamgbose (1966) and Givón (1990). In Vata, verbs can be clefted in the ways described above, as in

Vata (Koopman 1984: 38)

(158) *le* à le sàká

eat we eat rice

"It is eat that we eat rice / We are really **eating** rice."

In (158), the verb head *le* "eat" of the VP *le sákà* "eat rice" is fronted for clefting, leaving behind a copy in the VP. The fronted head does not show any nominal feature, compared with the cases in English, Yoruba, Berber, and Breton discussed in 4.3.2.1. The occurrence of the verb copy plays a crucial role in helping preserve the underlying logical structure of the sentence and facilitating the semantic interpretation and processing.

The same verb clefting pattern is demonstrated by the Kwa languages of the Niger-Congo family (Givón 1990: 732), which show nominal features of clefted verbs as well as the verb retention strategy. For example, Yoruba, a language spoken mainly in Nigeria with a basic word order of SVO, exhibits such verb clefting features as well as structural evidence for NPs in support of the Cleftability Hierarchy. In Yoruba, the cleft focus occurs initially, followed by the CFM *ni* or *lo* which is identical in form to a copula. Among the cleftable constituents, as exemplified below, are subjects (159b), direct objects (160b), oblique NPs (161), genitive NPs (162), and VP heads (163).

Yoruba (Bamgbose 1966)

(159) a. oló. run jé oba

God is king

"God is a king."

b. *oló. run* (*ló* jé) oba

God CFM is king

"It's God that is a king."

(160) a. wón ra-so

they bought-dress

"They bought a dress."

b. *aso* *(*ni*) wón rà

dress CFM they bought

"It was a dress that they bought."

(161) *àdá* *(*ni*) wón fi ge

matchet CFM they with cut-it

"It was a matchet that they cut it with."

(162) *bàbá. mi* *ni*-lé èé wó
father my is house his collapsed
"It was my father whose house collapsed."

(163) a. *gbí-gbé* *(*ni*) wón gbé e lo
carry-carry CFM they carried it go
"It's carrying that they carried it off."

b. *kpe-kpe* *(*ni*) ajá kpa adìe (Givón 1990:732)
kill-kill CFM dog kill chicken
"It's killing that the dog did to the chicken."
(lit. "It's killing that the dog killed the chicken.")

With regard to clefting strategies, it is noted that the retention strategy is used only when the cleft focus is a genitive NP or a verb, both having very low cleftability. According to Criterion (17b) of Chapter 2 concerning deletion versus retention, the scale of cleftability in Yoruba may be shown as SU = DO = Obl > Gen = V, with the constituent IO presumably collapsed with oblique NPs. The pattern conforms to the Cleftability Hierarchy, or at least does not violate it.

Another observation from the above data, the significance of which is not yet clear, is that while the CFM in all other cases is obligatory, with subject clefting, as in (159b), it is optional. Also, while in all other cases the CFM is identical with the copular form *ni*, with subject clefting, the CFM takes the copular form *ló*. One may surmise that such formal differences may have something to do with different degrees of cleftability between subjects and non-subjects, in the general sense that the easier to cleft, the more unmarked. However, since no specific link is clear at this point, the implications of such differences in relation to cleftability remain to be explored.

In terms of verb clefting exemplified in (163), in addition to the verb copy which occurs in the V^0 position of the presupposed clause, the clefted verb also takes on nominal morphology through reduplication, a nominalizing process that makes a verbal noun out of a verb in Yoruba. Thus, the nominalization strategy for VP clefting as used in English, Berber, Breton and Hausa and the verb retention strategy as used in Vata are both used in Yoruba verb clefting.

A slightly different case is found in Haitian where the two strategies are used paradigmatically, i. e. either VP nominalization or verb retention is available, but they do not coexist in the same cleft sentence. For example,

Haitian (Lumsden & Lefebvre 1990)

(164) *se* *achte* li te achte flè yo
that/CFM buy he PST buy flower PL
"It is buy that he bought flowers."

(165) *se* *vini* *li* *a* Jan te fè
that/CFM come his DET John PST do/make
"It's his visit that John did."

In (164) the initial clefted verb has the same morphological form as the verb copy in the presupposed clause, and no structural clues suggest its nominalization. In (165), the fronted cleft focus does not leave behind a verb copy, and behaves like a nominal, which is seen in the following structural characteristics (Lumsden & Lefebvre 1990):

a) The clefted VP can cooccur, as in (165), with a determiner *a*, and/or a possessive marker *li* in the same phrase;

b) The predicate verb in the presupposed clause is *fè* "do/make" that normally subcategorizes for a following object NP, which is the cleft focus *vini* "com (ing)" in (165);

c) The cleft focus can cooccur with the particle *ki* "what", which is usually used with NPs, as in (166):

(166) se ki vini Jan ap fè?
CFM what come John ASP do
"What visit is it that John is doing?" (- a visit to dine or to pay a debt)

Typologically, then, we may say that theoretically, a language may opt to use different VP clefting strategies available to it or different combinations of such strategies. For example, while Hausa and Vata respectively use the VP nominalization strategy and verb retention strategy only, Yoruba uses both in the same cleft construction, and Haitian uses either. What is common between these different manifestations of clefting strategies, however, is that they all help render the cleft structure semantically more transparent and therefore easier for processing.

4.3.3 The Specificity Condition revisited: English

In 4.2.4, we summarized that predicative APs may be cleftable if they meet the Specificity Condition by taking on nominal properties, having a contrastive reading, and/or having a restrictive modifier of some kind. From the above discussion, we find that the first two characteristics are also true of VP clefting, i. e. the clefted VP in most cases exhibits nominal properties morpho-syntactically, and has contrastive reading. In the following discussion, it will be shown that VP cleftability can also be increased by using restrictive modifiers like adverbials, as is the case with English.

In English, we find ungrammatical sentences like (167a) with a clefted bare verb:

(167) a. * It is sit that he does. (Bolinger 1972:113)

b. ?? It is sit that he does best.

(167a) would be much more acceptable if the clefted verb were a nominal *-ing* form; the bare verb as it is in (167a) is uncleftable. However, according to Bolinger (1972), clefting of the verb is made possible "by adding a complement" (p. 113), so that the pro-form, *do*, appears less like an auxiliary, which is exemplified in (167b). Given that (167a) and (167b) present a kind of minimal pair in which the only distinct part is the absence versus presence of the adverb *best*, the difference in grammaticality and cleftability is clearly attributed to the use of the adverb, which semantically restricts the domain of the predicate and therefore makes it more specific. Thus we see that what characterize the specificity of clefted APs apply equally well to clefted VPs. All these, as indicated earlier, are various manifestations of the Nouniness Principle.

4.3.4 Summary

In sum, VP clefting, much like AP clefting, follows the Nouniness Principle by showing, in most cases, nominal features of the clefted verbal elements, endowing the cleft focus with a contrastive reading, and making the clefted constituent more specific with restrictive modifiers.

4.4 PP Clefting

4.4.1 Proposition-internal and proposition-external PPs

Following Delahunty (1984), PP adverbials in this study refer to prepositional phrases used as adverbials, NP adverbials and clausal adverbials. It is generally observed that unlike APs and VPs, which normally have very low cleftability, PP adverbials enjoy high cleftability crosslinguistically, as evident in English (2.5.1), Tera (2.4.5), Malagasy (2.2.1.4), Mandarin Chinese (3.2.1), Danish (NØlke 1984), and crosslinguistic frequency comparison between adverbial and NP clefting (2.5.2). A closer examination of PP clefting, however, reveals that not all PP adverbials are equally cleftable; in fact, cleftability among PP adverbials can vary to such an extent that some may have high cleftability only next to subject on the Cleftability Hierarchy, while others may not be cleftable at all. For example, in English we find the following possibilities for PP clefting (Delahunty 1984:75):

(168) a. It was to Mary that Bill offered the chastity belt.
b. It was for Cynthia that Fred thought of buying the baby grand.
c. It was by the Gauls that Rome was sacked in 387 B. C.
d. It was with a knife that George attempted to slice the salami.
e. It was with Fred that we went to the movie.
f. It was in the hallway that we waited.
g. It was out of an underground passage that he appeared.
h. It was up to the microphone that Kenneth strode.
i. It was at three o'clock that he showed up.

The cleft focus is dative in (168a), benefactive in (168b), agentive in (168c), instrumental in (168d), accompaniment in (168e), locative in (168f), path in (168g), directive in (168h), and temporal in (168i). Thus English seems to allow for a large set of PP foci ranging over the entire paradigm of semantic roles and functions possible for the category PP, be they subcategorized, as in (168a), or adverbial. This is compounded by their high frequency of occurrence as cleft foci, demonstrated in Collins' (1987) quantitative study, in which PP clefting frequency is 21.5%, next only to subject NP clefting (50.4%), and in my crosslinguistic survey (2.5.2), with adverbial clefting found in 68% of the 40 languages examined.

On the other hand, we find totally uncleftable PPs such as the following:

(169) a. * It is to my mind that he is a genius.
b. * It is in fact that people follow grammatical rules when they speak.

A similar situation exists in Danish, where cleftability shows a three-way distinction between cleftable, uncleftable and questionably cleftable PP adverbials (NØlke 1984; C. Reinholtz p. c.):

Danish

(170) a. Det var kl. 3, SØren sagde, han ville komme hjem.
it was clock 3 Soren said 3s would come home
"It was at three o'clock that Soren said he would come home."
b. Det var i Frankrig, SØren var sidste sommer.
it was in France Soren was last summer
"It was in France that Soren was last summer."

(171) ? Det var med en hammer, Peter sagde, han ville sla lasen op.
it was with a hammer Peter said 3s would break lock up
"It was with a hammer that Peter said he would break up the lock."

(172) * Det var til min overraskelse, at Peter havde gjort det.
it was to my surprise that Peter have done it
" * It was to my surprise that Peter had done it."

According to NØlke (1984), sentences like (170), where the cleft focus is an adjunct of time or location, are grammatical, those like (172) totally unacceptable, and those like (171) sound a little odd. In his opinion, in Danish all clefts with focused PPs or adverbs "denoting other things than time and place" are only questionably cleftable (p. 90), which seems to rank locative/temporal PPs high on the Hierarchy.

On the surface, sentences like (168) and (170) formally resemble those like (169) and (172): both have PPs in cleft focus that function as adverbials. A closer scrutiny, however, reveals that they are two quite different kinds of adverbials, which is shown in a number of important ways.

Discourse-pragmatically, the function of the PPs in (168) and (170) is to modify or qualify the main predication and therefore can be said to be proposition-internal. In other words, they restrictively modify the proposition expressed by the clause. We may call such adverbials proposition-internal adverbials or simply adjuncts (Quirk et al. 1985). On the other hand, the function of the PPs in (169) and (172) is not to modify or qualify the proposition expressed by the clause, but to modify or qualify the speech act which the speaker is performing in uttering the clause. They can be termed proposition-external or speaker-oriented adverbials (Jackendoff 1972; Thompson & Langacre 1985), or simply disjuncts (Quirk et al. 1985).

The distinction between proposition-internal and proposition-external adverbials is justified by a number of structural properties which, among other things, include the following:

(i) proposition-internal, but not proposition-external, PPs can be contrasted with another adverbial in alternative interrogation, as in (173a) and (173b), respectively;

(ii) proposition-internal, but not proposition-external, PPs fall in the scope of negation, as in (174), where (174a) is ungrammatical because the adjunct as part of a negated predication is outside of the scope of negation by virtue of occurring initially;

(iii) Most proposition-internal PPs can be substituted with a WH-word in WH-questions, whereas proposition-external PPs can not.

(173) a. Did you see him in the library or in the cafeteria?

b. * Is he a genius to your mind or to her mind?

(174) a. * At a slow pace he didn't do it.

b. In my opinion, he didn't do it.

Semantically, proposition-internal and proposition-external PPs differ as to whether some semantic role is identifiable with a PP. While the former usually have a semantic role (locative, instrumental, etc.) associated with certain grammatical case, this is not the case with the latter. In other words, proposition-internal PP adjuncts can be treated as adverbial arguments with thematic roles, whereas proposition-external PPs are not arguments.

The pragmatic and semantic differences between the two kinds of PPs are reflected in the different ways they are represented structurally. According to Jackendoff (1972) and Heggie (1988), a proposition-external PP should attach to IP, i.e. a sister to VP; whereas a proposition-internal PP should attach to VP, as a sister to V^0 or V'. Thus their argument versus non-argument status is represented through their respective closeness to the verb head.

4.4.2 PP clefting and the Nouniness Principle

With respect to cleftability, the point is simply this: *A more argument-like PP will be more cleftable*. This is borne out by the additional evidence that even a locative PP in the post-copula predicational position, a non-argument position, is normally not cleftable, just like predicational APs or NPs. This is shown in sentences like * *It's at home that he is*. Since arguments are typically assumed by NPs, a reasonable conclusion seems to be that proposition-internal PPs tend to be cleftable because they are a kind of argument and therefore are noun-like. In fact, a similar treatment can be found in Ross (1967: 13), in which prepositions are considered only as a kind of appendix to the NP, despite the important and unique role PPs play in syntax.

Crosslinguistically, many languages (e.g. Turkish and Russian) express semantic roles such as locative and instrumental in the form of an NP plus some affix which is functionally equivalent to a preposition or postposition. In such languages, the case markers are incorporated into the NP, and the resulting structure resembles that of a genitive NP in English (e.g. *the boy*'s *pet*). This resemblance in structure, plus the more important aspect of case roles, enables us to treat PP adjuncts or PP-like structures as NP-like arguments.

If the above argument is accepted, then we can say that the Nouniness Principle also provides an account for PP clefting along the following line: PP arguments are NP-like and therefore are more cleftable; whereas non-argument PPs are not cleftable.

4.5 ADVP clefting

The adverb phrases we are considering in this section are those which function as adverbials in a sentence, rather than modifiers such as *extremely* in *He did extremely well*.

Generally, such ADVPs are not highly cleftable except those of time and location. Intra-categorially, however, clefting of ADVPs presents a kind of hierarchy or continuum whereby ADVPs of different kinds range from the more cleftable to the less cleftable depending on a number of factors. The following sentences from English exemplify this (Heggie 1988):

(175) a. It was then that she finally made up her mind.

b. ?? It was slowly that John closed the door and got back to work.

c. ?* It was usually that he had noodles for breakfast.

d. * It was probably/possibly that the rain damaged the roofs.

The cleft foci in the above sentences are all adverbs ending in *-ly* except in (175a); however, they differ in degree of grammaticality: according to Heggie (1988), (175a) is fully grammatical, (175b) questionable, (175c) problematic, and (175d) totally ungrammatical.

Similar distinctions are observed in other languages as well, for example, in

Danish (NØlke 1984):

Danish (NØlke 1984: 84)

(176) a. Det var (forst) derefter, de forstod det.
it was only after 3PL understood it
"It was (only) afterwards (that) they understood it."

b. ? Det var venligt, han sagde, hun burde behandles.
it was kindly he said she should be = treated
"It was kindly (that) he said she ought to be treated."

c. * Det er heldigvis, Peter er kommet tilbage.
it is fortunately Peter has come back
"It is fortunately that Peter has come back."

In the Danish data, (176a) is fully grammatical; (176b), questionable; and (176c), ungrammatical. Thus it can be seen that the differences of cleftability between different kinds of ADVPs in these languages in a way parallel those of PP clefting (4.4). The question is: what is it that determines cleftability of an adverbial ADVP, and how is ADVP cleftability related to the Nouniness Principle? A possible answer involves, among other things, the semantic closeness with which an adverbial is related to the verb, or to the action, event or state expressed by the verb.

To begin with, we can distinguish, as we did with PP clefting, between two kinds of adverbial phrases on pragmatic grounds, *viz.* speaker-oriented disjuncts and subject-oriented adjuncts. To recapitulate, speaker-oriented disjuncts (Quirk et al. 1985) or adverbials (Jackendoff 1972; Thompson & Longacre 1985) comment on the content of the communication without modifying the proposition *per se* (Quirk et al. 1985). For example, the attitudinal disjuncts *probably/possibly* in (175d) simply express the speaker's comment on the extent to which s/he believes what s/he is saying is true. On the other hand, subject-oriented adjuncts, such as those in (175a-c), function to modify or qualify the main predication and therefore can be viewed as being proposition-internal and having a closer semantic relationship with the verb.

The distinction between speaker-oriented and subject-oriented adverbials enables us to make the following descriptive statement about ADVP cleftability which accounts for the difference between (175a-c) and (176a-b) on the one hand and (175d) and (176c) on the other:

Subject-oriented adverbials are cleftable, whereas speaker-oriented adverbials are not.

The underlying motivation for this, it is contended, is the semantic domain of cleft sentences, *viz*, clefting involves only proposition-bound constituents. Since the proposition-bound properties of clefting will be discussed in detail in 5.2, suffice it to say here that because speaker-oriented adverbials are proposition-external, they are not cleftable.

As shown in (175), clefting of single adverbs ending in *-ly* seems to cause problems, which view is also expressed in Delahunty (1984), Heggie (1988), and Smits (1989). However, if these adverbs are modified by restrictive modifiers such as the delimiter *only*, the result is much more acceptable:

(177) a. ? It was slowly that Mary dressed to go out. (Delahunty 1984:80)

b. It wasn't only slowly that Mary dressed, but carefully too.

(178) a. ?? It's reluctantly that we agreed to swim.

b. It's only reluctantly that we agreed to swim at all.

(Heggie 1988: 226, cited from Pinkham & Hankamer 1975)

As Smits (1989: 300) points out, the use of delimiters like *only* has the effect of attaching to the focused part a sense of exclusiveness, which, as in the case of VP clefting, is probably what is responsible for the increased cleftability. Moreover, given that proposition-internal PPs are case-marked and argument-like (4.4), the fact that proposition-bound adverbs are more easily replaceable by PPs (e.g. *at that time* for *then*; *in a slow manner* for *slowly*) than disjunct adverbs (e.g. * *in a probable way* for *probably*) might be indicative of the former's greater degree of nouniness. In that sense, the Nouniness Principle can perhaps account for the different degrees of cleftability between proposition-internal and proposition-external ADVPs, albeit in an indirect way.

4.6 Summary and Conclusion

In this chapter, we have examined non-NPs as a possible, different domain to which the Cleftability Hierarchy may apply. An initial critique of the Cleftability Hierarchy reveals that the Hierarchy in its original form has its applicability limited to only NP arguments. To accommodate non-NPs, the Cleftability Hierarchy has at least to be supplemented by a context-dependent Nouniness Principle which, among other things, entails a Specificity Condition and which also interacts with other factors such as the clefting strategies (17b) and the distribution factor (17c). The non-NP categories examined include predicative APs, VPs, adverbial PPs, and ADVPs, all of which are susceptible to the Nouniness Principle in one way or another and to different extent when being clefted. Therefore, we may conclude that the Nouniness Principle not only quite adequately describes, but also explains, cleftability of non-NPs.

However, there are still some questions for which neither the Cleftability Hierarchy nor the Nouniness Principle seems to provide answers. Inter-categorially, neither can explain why some PP adjuncts (e. g. of time or place) are more easily cleftable than most kinds of NPs such as DO, IO and OBL, given that these NPs are at least as "nouny" as, and presumably more central arguments than, the PPs. Intra-categorially, neither can explain why some PP adjuncts are more cleftable than others, for example, why a locative PP is more cleftable than a dative PP in many languages despite the fact that the latter is subcategorized by the verb head but the former is not. Given these inadequacies, it seems that some account other than the Cleftability Hierarchy and the Nouniness Principle is needed to answer the above questions. Chapter 5 will approach the issue from a discourse-pragmatic perspective and try to come up with a general account of cleftability using the concept of thematicity.

Chapter 5 Towards a General Account of Cleftability

In Chapter 4, a nouniness principle is proposed as a complement to the Cleftability Hierarchy in accounting for cleftability of non-NP as well as NP constituents. For all the usefulness of the Nouniness Principle, its limitations in providing a full account of cleftability are noted. Since such an account is essential to an adequate grammar of cleft sentences, this chapter will focus on a proposed theory, *viz.* the Thematicity Principle, as a general account of cleftability, which not only subsumes both the Cleftability Hierarchy and the Nouniness Principle, but also answers questions raised at the end of Chapter 4 from a pragmatic point of view, questions that concern high cleftability of adjuncts of time and location in particular.

Since the Thematicity Principle to be proposed involves the crucial concept of *theme* and relates it to cleftability in important ways, a preliminary discussion of its theoretical background is in order. Therefore, we will first provide background information on *theme* and *thematicity* and discuss the pragmatic function of cleft sentences as it relates to theme, and then formally state the Thematicity Principle. Finally, empirical evidence from a study on a frequency of occurrence scale of thematic potential will be presented in support of the Thematicity Principle.

5.1 Theme and Thematicity

5.1.1 Theme

The concept of *theme* stemmed from Prague School terminology and has been used rather extensively in the literature without reaching consensus. According to Halliday (1967, 1985), *theme* is functionally defined as the communicative "point of departure of the clause, that with which the clause is concerned" (1985: 38).

Structurally, theme is predominantly marked syntactically by initial position crosslinguistically, but may also be marked otherwise, for example, morphologically by a particle (as the Japanese *wa*), an enclitic, or an affix (as the Tagalog *-ang*), or even syntactically by what Chafe (1976) calls *antitopics*, which occurs in final position, as in Seneca. In addition, theme can be marked phonologically by a separate intonation contour, such as in Chinese, especially when it is an adverbial or a non-subject NP (Halliday 1985).

It follows from this view of theme that crosslinguistically theme is not restricted to initial position, but may be any clause constituent with appropriate intonation and/or morphological marking. Initial position is admittedly a major, or even the only, means whereby the function of theme is realized in many languages. However, this should not preclude other possible means of realizing theme. As Halliday points out (1985: 39), there are "other languages which have a category of Theme functionally similar to that of English but which nevertheless express it in quite a different way." The implication of this variation in relation to cleftability is that in some non-configurational languages in which the cleft focus does not occur initially, it may still have thematic force.

While Halliday rightly points out crosslinguistic variation of thematic realization, Chafe (1976) notes inadequacies of defining *theme* (what he calls *topic*) as "what the sentence is about," which "applies better to English subjects" (p. 50) but does not apply to external topics in topic-prominent languages like Chinese. Since the function of such a theme/topic is to limit the applicability of the main predication to a certain restricted domain, it is more appropriate to define it as that which "sets a spatial, temporal, or individual framework within which the main predication holds." (*ibid.*) Compared with Halliday's notion of theme, Chafe's definition seems to enjoy more crosslinguistic plausibility.

As reflected in Chafe's confluence of theme and topic, inconsistencies in using the two terms *theme* and *topic* have long been existed. Basically, the issue has to do with whether theme and topic are distinct semantico-pragmatic notions. To Chafe (1976), theme and topic are clearly not distinct categories, as seen in his consideration of *the play* in *The play, John saw yesterday* as the topic "or theme" in the Hallidayan sense (p. 49). Declerck (1984), likewise, does not seem to make a distinction between theme and topic, as seen in his referring to Givón's (1983) discussion of topicality as "another theory of theme/topic". (p. 278)

On the other hand, linguists like Dik (1980) distinguish between theme and topic by relating them to different structural configurations. According to Dik, a theme

> *specifies the universe of discourse with respect of which the subsequent predication is presented as relevant. It is assigned to constituents which precede the predication... [and] often presented in 'absolute' form, i. e. without any specified semantic or syntactic function.* (pp. 15-16)

This functional definition of theme is basically like Chafe's (1976), but Chafe's definition is more specific by virtue of mentioning "spatial, temporal, or individual framework."

On the other hand, topic is defined by Dik (1980: 16) as presenting "the entity about which the predication predicates something in the given setting. Topic is assigned to constituents of the predication proper," where "predication" is interpreted as "proposition." Compared with theme, topic has a more limited scope in that it has to function within the setting defined by theme. In fact, Dik's distinction between theme and topic coincides with Foley and Van Valin's (1985) distinction between external topic and subject, where the former is not a clause constituent and does not necessarily bear semantic relationship to the predicate or its arguments, whereas the latter is a basic NP constituent of the clause and must correspond to an argument of the verb semantically (p. 300). As will be seen in 5.2, this distinction plays a crucial role in adequately accounting for cleftability of various kinds of constituents.

As for Halliday himself, the difference between topic and theme is that topic is only one kind of theme, *viz.* topical theme, which is "the first element in the clause that has some function in the ideational structure (i. e. in transitivity)" (1985: 56). Topical theme is usually assumed by grammatical functions such as subject, object or a circumstantial adjunct. Because topic is only a subcategory of theme and does not treat "theme" and "given" as functionally distinct notions, Halliday considers theme a more appropriate term for his framework.

Given the multitude of such diversified use of the term *theme*, and possible confusion therefrom, *theme* will be operationally defined here as in (179):

(179) A theme is that which specifies a spatial, temporal, or individual framework with respect of which the subsequent predication is presented as relevant.

(179) as a functional definition of theme draws from both Chafe (1976) and Dik

(1980), for the obvious reason of crosslinguistic plausibility. Such a definition will be able to accommodate crosslinguistic variation by recognizing different formal possibilities of realizing a theme in different languages. In particular, this author will take the position that in most languages theme is identified by its occurrence in initial position, although some languages may express it through other means; and that thematicity as it relates to cleftability should be measured in terms of "thematic potential," which refers to degrees of potentiality for a grammatical function to serve as a spatial, temporal, or individual framework within which the main predication holds, and "thematic actual," defined as the actual occurrence of the cleft focus as theme in the preceding context. Finally, a continuum of markedness of thematicity will be assumed and, based on an examination of different grammatical functions in terms of their thematic potential and thematic actual, the term *unmarked theme* will be used to refer to theme assumed by subjects, and marked theme to refer to theme assumed by other grammatical functions down a thematicity scale, to which we now turn.

5.1.2 Thematicity

While theme can be said to be the *actual* discourse framework within which the main predication holds true, thematicity is defined as the *potential* for a clause constituent to act as theme. As Givón (1984: 137) notes, human discourse is "prototypically about the fate, affairs, doings, trials and tribulations of individual—most commonly nominal—topics." Potentially, all nominal arguments in propositions are topical in this sense, especially subjects, direct objects and indirect objects, which can be ranked in the order Subject > Direct Object > Indirect Object, according to their potential to code the most important, recurrent, and continuous topic. Presumably, much of what Givón says applies to thematicity. In discourse, we notice that theme is typically conflated with subject in the most common type of sentences, *viz*. declarative sentences. This we may call the unmarked theme. On the other hand, a theme which is realized by constituents other than subject, such as a direct or indirect object or an adjunct, may be called a marked theme. According to Halliday (1985: 45), "the most usual form of marked Theme is an adverbial group... functioning as ADJUNCT in the clause, [and] least likely to be thematic is a COMPLEMENT [= object]." Put together, then, the rank of thematicity of the different grammatical functions can be shown as: Subject > Adjunct > Direct Object >

Indirect Object. Halliday also notes thematicity of oblique NPs: "[S]ometimes even the Complement from within a prepositional phrase functions as Theme." (p. 45) Although not stated explicitly, it can be readily inferred that such oblique NPs have less thematic potential than direct and indirect objects. What is interesting from this comparison between Givón and Halliday is that while the former does not mention thematicity of adjuncts, the latter considers them as having high thematic potential, which view is echoed in Sanders (1984), Thompson and Longacre (1985), and Collins (1987), and attested by research results from Collin's (1987) study and from this author's own study to be reported in 5.4.

Part of the above scale, *viz.* Direct Object > Indirect Object, is supported by empirical evidence from Givón's (1982) textual comparison between direct and indirect objects in terms of their realizations by pronouns versus full NPs. The study takes the assumption that pronouns are more topical than full NPs because they are more continuous and persistent, and the results show that while nearly 90% of direct objects (N = 38) are realized by pronouns with only about 10% realized by full NPs, all the indirect objects (N = 7) are realized by full NPs. Although one may have concerns about the small number of observations (N = 7) obtained for indirect objects, the results in general support the claim that direct objects are more topical (in our case, more thematic) than indirect objects.

Now, if we assume that genitive NPs, which as non-heads have only quasi-argument status, have even less thematic potential, and other non-argument elements (e. g. adverb adjuncts, predicational elements, VPs) have still less thematic potential, in that order, then it is possible to posit a thematicity scale as in (180):

(180) **The Thematicity Scale**

SU > $\mathbf{ADJUNCT_{T/L}}$ > DO > IO > OBL NP > GEN NP > $\mathbf{ADJUNCT_{adv}}$ > PREDICATIVE > VP

(180) states that the grammatical positions toward the left on the scale tend to have greater thematic potential in discourse than those toward the right. In terms of markedness, the leftmost position will occur as the most unmarked theme, whereas the rightmost position as the most marked theme. The particular elements presented on the scale have been chosen in accordance with the grammatical functions examined so far. It should be noted that adjuncts of time and location, which can either be a PP, NP or adverbial clause, are ranked high in thematicity, as compared to adjuncts of other semantic roles, especially those realized by single adverbs. This is because

adjuncts of time and location in general have typical thematic properties and functions by virtue of occurring in initial position in many languages①, thus setting a temporal or spatial world for particular discourse that is taking place (Thompson & Longacre 1985), as shown in the following examples from Chafe (1976):

(181) a. Tuesday I went to the dentist.

b. In Dwinelle Hall people are always getting lost.

5.2 The Function of Clefts

5.2.1 Focused thematization

Given what has been said about theme and thematicity, we are now in a position to relate them functionally to cleftability. Functionally, it is generally believed that cleft sentences serve to contrastively focus on a clause constituent morpho-syntactically singled out for such prominence (Deng 1979), as mentioned in Chapter 1. Another way to look at the function of cleft sentences is in terms of the pragmatic notion of thematicity, as suggested in Prince (1978), Brömser (1984), Declerck (1984), Timm (1987), and Collins (1987, 1991).

While in non-cleft sentences, theme is usually some presupposed element, in cleft sentences, it is the focused element that functions as theme (Declerck 1984; Halliday 1985). What this means is that

(182) a. clefting is in some important way closely associated with thematization;

b. given the high cleftability of subjects and adjuncts (of time and location), it seems that the function of clefting is, among other things, to "imbue an already thematic element," or at least a potentially thematic element, with "further prominence" (Declerck 1984: 277) by focusing it; and

c. the effect of clefting is focused thematization (Brömser 1984).

(182a) has been noted in many languages, for instance English (Chomsky 1977), Kinyarwanda (Kimemyi 1978) where the Cleft 2 pattern contrastively focuses on a topicalized/thematized NP (2.4.4), and Ivatan (Reid 1966). In relation to

① Even in some non-configurational languages such as Chinese, where no dislocation is apparent in WH-questions, relativization and clefting (Huang 1982a), adjuncts may still be fronted as theme.

(182b) above, thematic prominence is generated through highlighting the theme part of a sentence, by means of predication in some languages such as English and French, fronting or extraposition in others, and morphological marking in still other languages such as Chinese. There are two ways whereby we can interpret thematic prominence: thematic potential and thematic actual, both being important aspects of identifying thematicity of the focused constituent in a cleft sentence. Thematic potential, as mentioned in 5.1.1, is the general statistical probability of a particular kind of focused grammatical function that can occur as theme in non-cleft sentences. Thematic actual, on the other hand, refers to the actual occurrence of the cleft focus as theme in the preceding context. For example, cleft focus in English and many other languages tends to be elements that continue the thematic line of the preceding discourse via various morphosyntactic devices. This view is in line with Givón's (1983) proposition that the focused element tends to be an "important topic," i.e. "a rather persistent topic in terms of the succeeding discourse context" (p. 265). This argument for high thematicity of cleft focus measured in terms of thematic actual is supported by empirical evidence, as seen in the following excerpt from an article on the former Prime Minister of Canada Kim Campbell in *the Toronto Star* (italics mine):

(183) ... I turn and bump into a rock: Pat Carney. *She*'s not smiling. The plot thickens.

... ...

Loyal British Columbian that *she* is, *Carney* does not support Campbell's leadership bid; there is no love lost between these two, but *Carney* will not speak about Campbell, except to explain *they* are related by marriage. *Carney*'s cousin Marguerite Parkinson is the third wife of George Campbell, Kim's father.

It was ***Carney***, the senator, who flew from Vancouver to Ottawa on Feb. 1, 1991, to cast the crucial vote (in a 43-43 tie) that killed Justice Minister Campbell's legislative effort to recriminalize abortion, making Carney a hero to a broad range of medical and feminist groups.

In (183), the italicized words mark the continued theme, *Carney*. As noticed, the cleft sentence appears in the last paragraph, with the proper noun *Carney* as the cleft focus. The same NP had been introduced into the discourse three paragraphs back and has persisted as theme throughout the paragraphs immediately preceding the cleft sentence before it becomes the cleft focus. Thus it is clear that what appears as the cleft focus continues the thematic line of the preceding discourse. A similar example is found in the same issue of *the Toronto Star*, in another article (Brennan 1993: E1):

(184) His partner in North Drive Estates is his 31-year-old son, *Danny*. *We*'ve been building homes together since *he* was a teenager.

It was *Danny* who found this site. I've driven past this corner hundreds of times but never paid any notice to it because you can't see anything for the trees... [italics mine]

Here again, the italicized words represent the continued theme, and it can be seen how the NP *Danny* persists as theme (or part of the theme) in the preceding text before it becomes the cleft focus. The two examples, then, clearly show high thematicity of the cleft foci as reflected in their thematic actual in the context.

Crosslinguistic data also provides empirical evidence for high thematicity of the cleft focus, for example, in the following excerpts from the works of two contemporary Chinese writers. For ease of exposition, and because word-for-word glossing is not crucial in analyzing the pragmatic structure here, only the translated texts have been presented here for analysis, which are kept as close as possible to the original grammatical and rhetorical structures [translation and italics mine].

(185) *Doctor Gu* took great care of me and Old Zhou. It was *he* who offered to lend us a share of his two bags of glucose powder... (Wang 1990: 227)

(186) *He* was a well-known expert on international issues, and had done quite a lot for the communists. It was *he* who organized the translation and publication of Snow's *Red Star Over China*. (Wang 1990: 240)

(187) After the "Cultural Revolution" had begun, these people turned the Duyong Village into a living hell. They searched houses and made arrests at will, and used more than twenty types of torture. During the daytime, numerous "criticism meetings" were held. At night, sounds of beating and swearing, screaming and howling of the tortured, and their relatives' crying filled the air... It was to such a (production) brigade that Zhang Shuqu was sent to do supervised hard labour. (Liu 1987: 6)

In both (185) and (186) from the same author, the cleft focus has occurred as theme in the immediately preceding context, thus continuing the thematic line of discourse. (187), on the other hand, has a circumstantial adjunct (i. e. the locative *to such a brigade*) as cleft focus, which had been introduced in the first sentence of the paragraph as the locative setting wherein various events are described to support the assertion that the village had become a "living hell". Compared with (185) and (186), the thematic line before the cleft focus in (187) is continued through whole-sentence descriptions of the setting rather than through the subject-theme as in (185) an (186). In all the cases, we see how clefting helps highlight theme in discourse. Thus, the crosslinguistic data shows "focused thematization" as a viable and plausible function of cleft sentences.

5.2.2 Clause binding and salient information

There is, however, a problem of underspecification with Brömser (1984), Declerck (1984), and Collins (1987), when they propose focused thematization as a distinct function of cleft sentences. Consider

(188) a. In the hallway, we waited.

b. It is in the hallway that we waited.

(189) a. As for the book, he's signed a contract with the publisher.

b. * It is as for the book that he's signed a contract with the publisher.

(190) a. ... these three little sisters, they were learning to draw.

b. * It is these three little sisters who_i $they_i$ were learning to draw.

By definition, *in the hallway* in (188a), *as for the book* in (189a), and *these three little sisters* in (190a) are all themes. If Brömser, Declerck and Collins were right, we would expect these themes to be all cleftable, because they are "already thematic". However, we find that only the theme in (188a) is cleftable, as in (188b); whereas the themes in (189a) and (190a) are not, as in (189b) and (190b), respectively. It seems, then, that not all elements that are already thematic in the discourse context are cleftable. Clearly, the thematization theory of Brömser (1984), Declerck (1984) and Collins (1987) overgenerates. The cause of the problem, it is argued here, is underspecification of the function of clefts, i. e. the theory does not adequately specify what kind(s) of theme can be cleft focused and what kind(s) can not. A closer look at (188) and (190) shows that the cleft focus in (188b) is a clause-internal constituent that participates in the transitivity or argument structure of (188a), in this case an adjunct of location. On the other hand, those in (189b) and (190b) do not participate in the transitivity or argument structure of (189a) and (190a), i. e. they are not part of the proposition *per se*.

This difference is recognized by Foley and Van Valin (1985) as topicalization versus left-dislocation (p. 355). However, to keep our terminology consistent, we will call the kind of theme in (188a) clause-internal theme, much like Halliday's (1985) topical theme, and those in (189a) and (190a) clause-external theme. This difference, along with the subsequent difference in cleftability, shows that clefting is proposition-bound, i. e., clefting affects only constituents with thematic force which are part of the proposition. Since the themes in (189a) and (190a) are both external themes, they can not be clefted. For the theory of cleftability to accommodate the above fact, it is suggested that "clause constituents" be specified in a statement of the function of clefts.

Another potential problem in stating the function of clefts is: how do we reconcile the apparent contradiction between thematicity, which is supposedly related to given information, and newness, both of which are supposedly embodied by the cleft focus? It is widely believed that the cleft focus tends to carry contrastive, new information (Collins 1987, 1991; Halliday 1985; Clark and Haviland 1977; Quirk et al. 1985; Prince 1978). Given what is said above about the function of cleft sentences, there seems, at first glance, to be some conflict between cleft focus as (new) information locus and cleft focus as that which has considerable thematic potential.

The answer, it is contended here, lies in how we interpret "new" in cleft focus. If we interpret the so-called new information embedded in cleft focus not as new because it is completely out of consciousness and unrecoverable from context, but as new because it fits the description in the presupposed part, i. e. as "newly identified or contrastive" (Collins 1987: 9), which singles out the correct and readily identifiable entity from a closed set of given possibilities, then we may say that such newness is in fact not contradictory to the concept of thematicity, in that the thematic element is originally part of the background, or "an exhaustive listing" (Chafe 1976), from which the focused item is identified and foregrounded. Evidence for this argument can be found in the tendency for cleft focus to be realized by anaphoric, deictic, or contrastive elements (Declerck 1984).

A more radical view is expressed by Chafe (1976: 35), who argued that the contrastive focus "does not—or need not" provide new information, simply because the Given-New distinction is not really relevant to contrastive sentences, of which clefts are a kind, where the focus may be given or new.

Given the above interpretation of newness, and given the possible irrelevance of newness in cleft sentences, it seems more appropriate to use what Geluykens (1991) calls *the most salient information* rather than new information to refer to the kind of information carried by cleft focus. Thus, to sum up, the function of cleft sentences can be stated as in (191):

(191) **The function of cleft sentences is to highlight clause-internal constituents which have relatively high thematic potential and/or which are actual themes in the proceeding discourse, and to highlight the most salient information in the clause.**

5.3 The Thematicity Principle (TP)

Considering the above discussion on theme, thematicity, and cleft functions, I will now propose the Thematicity Principle as follows:

(192) **The Thematicity Principle**

The more thematic a clause constituent is in non-clefts, the more cleftable it tends to be.

In (192), *thematic* refers to the potential for a clause constituent to be a clause-internal theme (or topical theme), which is realized prototypically by NP arguments and adjuncts (of time and location) and which basically excludes non-arguments and disjuncts, and downplays the role of constituents with semi-argument or quasi-argument status, as we noted earlier in this chapter as well as in Chapter 4. Also to be noted is the term *clause constituent*, which refers to constituents that participate in the transitivity or argument structure of a sentence, and properly excludes clefting of constituents which occur as clause-external theme, as we observed earlier. In this way, the Thematicity Principle captures an important distinction in the function of clefting, which is overlooked in Brömser (1984), Declerck (1984) and Collins (1987), where only general reference is made to "thematic" or "thematization" and overgeneralization ensues as a result.

The advantages of the Thematicity Principle over both the Cleftability Hierarchy and the Nouniness Principle are three-fold. Firstly, it is descriptively more adequate. Compared with the Cleftability Hierarchy, whose accountability is limited to NP constituents only, the Thematicity Principle accounts for both NP and non-NP cleftability. In terms of NPs, for example, it predicts greater cleftability of subjects than of other types of NPs because of the former's greater thematicity. In the same line, non-NP cleftability is also predicted; for example, PPs will be more cleftable than APs because of their argument or at least quasi-argument properties, and because arguments have greater thematic potential than non-arguments. In terms of PP clefting, the Thematicity Principle predicts that adjunct PPs of time and location not only have greater cleftability than other types of PP, but are more cleftable than some types of NPs, again because of their high thematic potential to serve as discourse setting. On the other hand, compared with the Nouniness Principle, which accounts for non-NP cleftability but can not cope with the relative degree of cleftability between different categories (e. g. some PPs are more cleftable than most NPs) nor with intra-categorial difference in cleftability (e. g. some PPs are more cleftable than others), the Thematicity Principle accommodates not only non-NPs but also such inter-categorial and intra-categorial differences with regard to cleftability. In a word, the Thematicity Principle not only subsumes what is accounted for by the Cleftability Hierarchy and the Nouniness Principle, but also accommodates what is not accountable by them.

Secondly, the Thematicity Principle is more explanatory. Although both the Cleftability Hierarchy and the Nouniness Principle appeal in some sense to a formal-functional account of cleftability, they do not do so in a direct way. For example, in answering why more noun-like elements are more cleftable, the Nouniness Principle will have to resort to argument status of the constituents concerned, which by itself does not provide a genuinely functional account; whereas the Thematicity Principle provides a direct answer: NP arguments are high in thematicity. In this sense, the Thematicity Principle provides a general and directly functional explanation of cleftability from the perspective of communicative functions.

Finally, this directness also points to a third advantage of the Thematicity Principle as a plausible theory: it has maximum simplicity, which is a desirable feature of a sound theory.

5.4 Further Empirical Evidence

An important feature of the Thematicity Principle is that the grammatical positions on the Thematicity Scale are rankable in a similar order to those of the Cleftability Hierarchy, and that the Thematicity Scale as presented in (180) subsumes the Cleftability Hierarchy in that it includes both NP and non-NP positions. So far we have presented extensive evidence in support of the Cleftability Hierarchy (Chapter 2), and some evidence in support of the Thematicity Principle (5.1.2, 5.2.1). Given the validity of the Cleftability Hierarchy, and given the expected correspondence between the Thematicity Scale and the Cleftability Hierarchy, one way to further validate the Thematicity Principle would be to see if empirical evidence can be found in actual discourse to show that the Thematicity Scale indeed correlates with the Cleftability Hierarchy. More specifically, if we find that the ratio of frequency of occurrence for different grammatical positions on the Thematicity Scale corresponds to the order of grammatical functions on the Cleftability Hierarchy, it would further support the Thematicity Principle.

A textual study was carried out in which sentences from two written texts are analyzed, counted and compared with regard to the ratio of different grammatical functions serving as topical themes in written discourse. The two texts represent two common genres of writing: a lengthy newspaper report from *Toronto Star* (Steed 1993) and four chapters① (Chapters 3-6) from a classical novel, *Alice in Wonderland*. The purpose of the study was to attest the hypothesis that in terms of frequency of occurrence, the relative order of grammatical functions as topical themes in non-clefts will correspond to that of grammatical functions as cleft foci in cleft sentences as proposed by the Thematicity Scale. Since the Thematicity Scale has been proposed as an extension of the Cleftability Hierarchy, the latter having been attested by extensive crosslinguistic evidence, the textual study only measures the frequency of occurrence of topical themes in non-clefts as mentioned above. Also, since topical theme concerns mainly NP arguments and adverbials (Halliday 1985), these are the focus of the textual study and their frequencies are counted as they occur in the texts. Thus, the categories under investigation include Subject, Direct Object, Indirect Object, Oblique Object, and Adjuncts, the last being further divided into adjuncts of time and location and adjuncts of other semantic roles, such as manner,

---

① The four chapters were randomly selected to ensure comparability in length with the other text.

condition and reason, to see if they differ in frequency of occurrence. As clauses, especially adverbial clauses, may be cleft foci themselves, sentence is used as the unit of measurement.

On the other hand, the following kinds of sentences are excluded from consideration: (i) sentences without explicit themes such as imperatives or verbless sentences (e.g. *Bang.*); (ii) Yes/No questions which start with a finite rather than topical theme; (iii) sentences with initial expletive forms such as *there* and non-referential *it*; and (iv) disjuncts. The main reason for excluding these types of constructions from consideration is relevancy: they are all without an initial, explicit topical theme.

The results of analysis are presented in Table 5.1 and Table 5.2, and graphically represented in Figure 5.1 and Figure 5.2, respectively. They show that subjects are by far the most frequent theme in both texts (78.9% and 75.1%, respectively), followed by adjuncts of time and location (13.5% and 17.7%, respectively), and then adjuncts of other semantic roles (5.7% and 6.9%, respectively). There are 7 instances (1.7%) of thematized direct objects in *Alice in Wonderland* and none in *the Toronto Star* report, probably due to stylistic difference between the two kinds of texts. Also, while no instance of thematized indirect object is found in either text, one instance of thematized oblique object is found in both texts. However, this difference is statistically insignificant.

Table 5.1 ***Comparison of frequency of occurrence for different grammatical positions as topical theme in Chapters 3-6 of Alice in Wonderland***

Function	Number of Occurrence	Percentage %
Subject	333	78.9
Adjunct: time/loc	57	13.5
other	24	5.7
Direct Object	7	1.7
Indirect Object	0	0
Oblique Object	1	0.2
Total	422	100

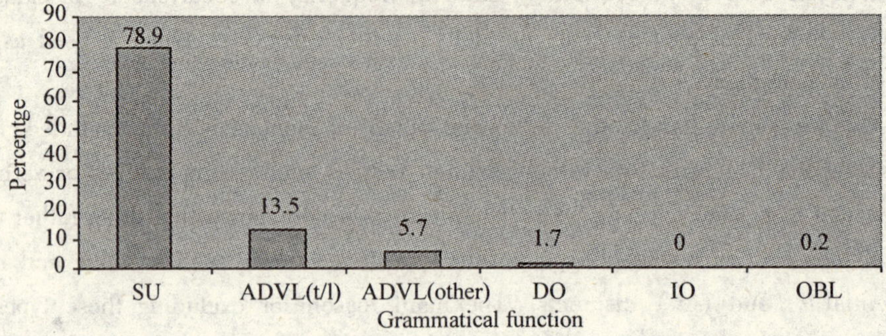

Figure 5.1 *Topical Themes in Alice in Wonderland: Frequency of Occurrence(%)*

Table 5.2 ***Comparison of frequency of occurrence for different grammatical positions as topical theme in a Toronto Star news report***

Function	Number of Occurrence	Percentage %
Subject	336	75.2
Adjunct: time/loc	79	17.7
other	31	6.9
Direct Object	0	0
Indirect Object	0	0
Oblique Object	1	0.2
Total	447	100

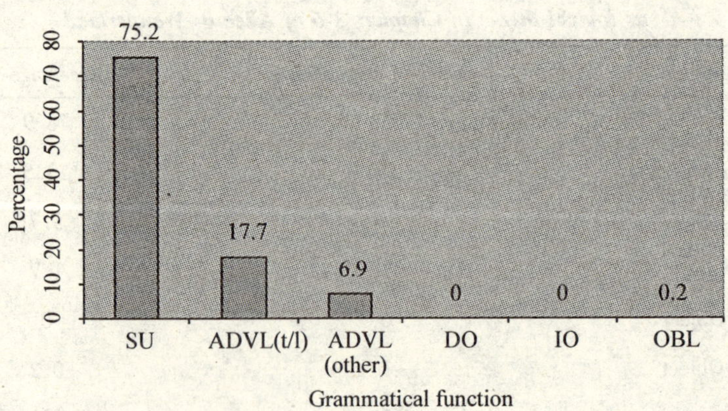

Figure 5.2 *Topical Themes in a Toronto Star Report: Frequency of Occurrence(%)*

To find out if and to what extent the results from the two texts correlate with each other in general, the Pearson Product Moment correlation test was performed to test the hypothesis that there is a significant correlation between the two sets of frequency counts. The results show a correlation coefficient of .99 at $p \leqslant .001$ (1-tailed significance), suggesting that there is a very significant correlation between the frequency counts of the two texts, and that stylistic difference probably plays a minor role in using the Thematicity Principle to account for cleftability of different grammatical positions.

On the whole, the thematic scale as attested in both texts can be shown as

(193) **SU > ADJUNCT$_{\textbf{time/loc}}$ > ADJUNCT$_{\textbf{other}}$ > DO > IO = OBL**

(193) corresponds to the order on the Cleftability Hierarchy as far as NP positions are concerned, and ranks thematicity of adjuncts between subjects and other NP positions, as predicted by the Thematicity Scale presented in (180). In general, therefore, the results of the textual study lend further support to the Thematicity Principle, in that more thematic constituents tend to have higher cleftability.

5.5 Summary

A Thematicity Principle is proposed in this chapter which attributes higher cleftability to higher thematicity, to account for cleftability of various grammatical functions in general. By defining theme as that which specifies a spatial, temporal or individual framework for the subsequent discourse, thematicity of various grammatical functions may be measured in terms of thematic potential and/or thematic actual, and presented on a thematicity scale that subsumes, and corresponds to the order of, the NP positions on the Cleftability Hierarchy. A crucial difference between the Thematicity Scale and the Cleftability Hierarchy (Chapter 2) or the Nouniness Principle (Chapter 4) is that the former, by referring to higher thematicity of adjuncts, especially adjuncts of time and location, makes it possible to account for higher cleftability of adjuncts of time and location in terms of the Thematicity Principle; whereas neither the Cleftability Hierarchy nor the Nouniness Principle can provide a full account. Given that the function of clefting is to highlight clause-bound constituents with relatively high thematic potential or thematic actual, evidence in support of the Thematicity Principle is of two kinds: qualitative and quantitative. Qualitatively, crosslinguistic examples from discourse texts show that the cleft focus tends to carry on the thematic line of the discourse by focusing on elements which are used as theme in the (immediately) preceding context. Quantitatively, results from a textual study show correspondence between the Thematicity Scale and the Cleftability Hierarchy in terms of the ordering of relevant grammatical positions, suggesting correlations between thematicity and cleftability, as proposed in the Thematicity Principle, (192). Therefore, the Thematicity Principle is considered superior to either the Cleftability Hierarchy or the Nouniness Principle in descriptive adequacy, explanatory adequacy, and simplicity, although the latter are valid in their respective domains.

Chapter 6 The Contrastive Focus Marker

6.1 Introduction

In the previous chapters, we examined cleftability of various grammatical positions with regard to three theories: the Cleftability Hierarchy, which is based on Keenan and Comrie's Accessibility Hierarchy, the Nouniness Principle, and the Thematicity Principle. It has been shown that while the Cleftability Hierarchy and the Nouniness Principle both work well within certain domains, the Thematicity Principle is acclaimed as the most descriptive and explanatory of the three.

Throughout the study on cleftability, various structural properties of cleft sentences have been examined crosslinguistically, such as those pertaining to movement, the clefting strategy, the contrastive focus marker, etc. Some of these structural properties are of special typological importance or exhibit workings of certain language universals such as the iconicity principle (Haiman 1985). To further pursue such aspects of the study, this chapter examines in some detail an important structural-functional constituent of cleft sentences, *viz.* the contrastive focus marker (CFM), in particular its formal identity and functional relationship to deictic pronouns and the copula. The findings will support a functional-iconic view of language.

6.2 Formal Identity between the CFM, the Copula and the Demonstrative

Grammaticalization often involves functional shift of the same form through reanalysis, etc., resulting in formal identity between coexisting grammatical categories. Such formal identity tends to be underlied by semantico-functional similarity between the categories concerned, especially when recurrent in diverse languages. This polysemy among syntactic categories differs from true homonymy in which formal identity is accidental. Studies on polysemy include Schachter (1973) on relative clauses and clefts, Keenan & Hull (1973) on indirect questions and relative clauses, Langacker & Munro (1975) on reflexives and passives, Haiman (1985) on conditional protases and polar questions, Stein (1988) on English person endings and the periphrastic *do*, Croft (1990) on directional and recipient *to* in English, and McWhorter (1994) on diachrony involving focus marker and copula in Swahili, to name a few.

In general, grammatical polysemy may be considered a kind of meta-iconic isomorphism, where one form is preserved for one (general) meaning or discourse function (Bolinger 1977: x). According to Haiman (1985), isomorphism is iconic by virtue of relating one form to one meaning/function, and polysemy is a form of isomorphism by virtue of associating like forms with like meanings or functions. However, given that iconicity and economy are two competing motivations for linguistic forms (Haiman 1985), questions arise as to whether it is possible for grammatical polysemy to be motivated by both forces, and how such compromise is achieved.

This chapter attempts to answer these questions by examining polysemy among demonstratives (DEM), copulas (CPL), and contrastive focus markers (CFM) used in clefts. As noted in Chapter 1, the cleft construction in many languages resembles, but is not exactly the same as, an equational sentence, with the configuration

(194) $[_S \langle Cpl \rangle X''_i \langle Cpl \rangle [_{S'} (Comp) [_S \ldots [_{x''_i} \underline{e}] \ldots]]]$

In (194), X''_i represents a left-dislocated XP for contrastive focusing which is marked by an adjacent form that is identical to a copula (Cpl) to its left or right depending on the canonical syntactic order of a language. The contrastive focus along with its marker is followed by a sub-clause (S') headed by a Comp(lementizer) wherein the trace (x''_i $\underline{e}$) marks the extraction site out of which the X''_i has been moved. Such a configuration is attested in languages such as English, Irish, and Breton:

<u>English</u>

(195) It ***is*** *the cat* that killed the bird.

<u>Irish</u> (McCloskey 1979)

(196) ***Is*** *é Seán aL thigeann 'na bhaile*
CPL him John that come home
"It's John that comes home."

Breton (*Timm* 1987)

(197) un hunvre eo ***ho*** peus bet.
a dream CPL 2PL-have had
"It's a dream that you had."

While it is true that contrastive focus in these languages is marked mainly by the structural configuration, the adjacent copula also helps mark the focus. Without the copula, a cleft sentence without a Comp heading the presupposed clause, as would be in (197), would be indistinguishable from other constructions such as one with a topicalized NP. Therefore, the copula thus used functions at least in part as a contrastive focus marker.

The focus-marking function of the copula-like form is more clearly seen in non-configurational languages with no overt movement for clefting, where the contrastive focus occurs in the same position as in a corresponding non-cleft sentence:

Chinese

(198) wo ***shi*** *zuotian* kanjian ta de.
I CPL/CFM yesterday see he MM
"It was yesterday that I saw him."
我是昨天看见他的。

Mopun (Frajzyngier 1987)

(199) n-kwat ***a*** *sii siwol.*
1S-pay CPL/CFM with money
"It is with money that I paid."

As pointed out in Chapter 1, the copula-like particle (*shi* in (198) and *à* in (199)) thus used is different from those in (195-197) in that the focus remains an argument within a one-clause structure. Consequently, the CFM is much less verb-like than in languages such as English and French. Crucially, the cleft reading would be lost without the presence of the copula-like CFM in (198) and (199).

There are still other languages where the form of the CFM appears to be associated more with that of a demonstrative pronoun than of a copula, as in (200)-(201).

Hebrew

(200) *ze* *ani* she-pihakti.
DEM/CFM I who yawned
"It is I who yawned."

Margi (Hoffmann 1963)

(201) *ni -ŋ* atsianyi.
I this kill-him
"It is I who killed him."

As will be shown, some of these languages (e. g. Mandarin Chinese, Hebrew and Margi) also exhibit formal identity or similarity between the CFM, the copula and the demonstrative pronoun in one way or another, which begs the question whether there is a common linguistic function that underlies these grammatical categories, and if so how we account for the polysemy in terms of iconicity and economy.

The remaining part of this chapter will address these issues by examining the presumably close formal relationship between the CFM, the copula and the demonstrative, in an attempt to explore a unitary functional account of such relationship. The theoretical framework used is basically functional, with special reference to some iconicity principles such as the isomorphism principle proposed in Haiman (1985), and the principle of semantic similarity which motivates cross-categorial formal identity as discussed in Stein (1988). It will be shown that linguistic change in morpho-syntax of a language can involve transfer of the same form from one category to another, transfer which is often motivated and conditioned by semantico-functional similarity between the linguistic categories involved. Such formal identity is often reflected synchronically through formal identity among coexisting categories. It will be contended that cross-categorial formal identity can be motivated by semantico-functional similarity, which proposition will be supported and gain potential universality if the same phenomenon is found crosslinguistically, especially in unrelated languages. To that end, crosslinguistic data were collected and examined from a number of languages, including Chinese, Hebrew, Margi, Mokilese, Kusaiean, and Malayalam. It will be shown that the grammatical categories in these unrelated languages all involve intercategorial transfer of the same form, which is characterized by functional similarity among the categories and motivated by both iconicity and economy. To start with, let us examine the form *shi* in Mandarin Chinese.

6.3 Polesemy in Mandarin Chinese

As shown in (198), the CFM in modern Chinese is *shi*, which is identical in form with the copula used in equational sentences like (202) with nominal predicates:

(202) Zhang San shi ta-de didi.
Zhang San CPL 3s-GEN younger-brother
"Zhang San is his younger brother."
张三是他的弟弟。

This same form was initially used as a demonstrative in Archaic Chinese (11th c. — 3rd c. BC), whose remnants can still be seen in some quite pedantic expressions in Modern Chinese:

(203) a. shi ke-ren, shu bu ke-ren
DEM tolerable what not tolerable
"(If) this is tolerable, what (is) not tolerable?"
是可忍,孰不可忍?

b. shi ri
DEM day
"that day"
是日

Given that the CFM, the copula verb and the demonstrative all use the same form, there are at least three possible explanations for this formal identity:

(204) a. it is a mere coincidence;
b. the forms are diachronically related;
c. the forms have a common pragmatic function.

(204a) is untenable before we have had to reject (203b) and (203c). To examine (204b) and (204c), we begin with the following hypotheses:

(205) a. The diachronic change for *shi* is: demonstrative > copula > CFM.
b. The demonstrative, the copula and the CFM all share a common pragmatic function.

6.3.1 Synchronic evidence

(205a) presupposes some intercategorial diachronic relationship between the demonstrative, the copula and the CFM, and suggests a closer diachronic relationship between the demonstrative *shi* and the copula *shi* in Chinese. One piece of synchronic evidence in support of this claim is that in Chinese, the copula *shi* is in general subject to the same structural constraint as the demonstrative pronoun *shi* in its determiner use, i. e. normally it can only occur before an NP (cf. Hashimoto 1969), whereas the CFM *shi* can occur before non-NPs as well as NPs. Compare the following examples:

(206) a. ta shi xuesheng.
3s CPL student
"He is a student."
他是学生。
b. *ta shi hao / chi fan / cong Meiguo.
3s CPL kind eat meal from U. S. A.
"He is kind/eating/from the U. S. A."
*他是好 / *他是吃饭 / *他是从美国。

(207) a. *shi wo* zuotian zai jie-shang kanjian ta de.
CFM 1s yesterday LOC street-on see 3s MM
"It is I who saw him on the street yesterday."
是我昨天在街上看见他的。
b. wo zuotian *shi zai jie-shang* kanjian ta de.
1s yesterday CFM LOC street-on see 3s MM
"It is on the street that I saw him yesterday."
我昨天是在街上看见他的。

In (206), *shi* is used as a copula, which is normally not stressed and should occur before nominal predicates. (206b) is ungrammatical due to the presence of the copula before a non-NP. In (207), however, *shi* is used as a CFM, which can appear before non-NPs as well as NPs, usually with some additional stress on the focused NP or PP or on itself if the focus is an AP or VP.

There are some apparent counterexamples to the constraint that the copula *shi* appears only before NPs. First, consider (208), where *shi* appears before an AP/VP and is stressed:

(208) a. ta ***shí*** (hen) hao.
3s CPL very kind
"He is indeed (very) kind."
他是(很)好。

b. ta ***shí*** qu-guo Jia'nada.
3s CPL go-PERF Canada
"He's indeed been to Canada."
他是去过加拿大。

If *shi* were the copula, the fact that it appears before an AP and a VP respectively in the grammatical sentences (208a) and (208b), would be a violation of the aforementioned constraint. However, it is argued here that *shi* should be analyzed not as copula but as CFM (cf. EMPH marker in Chomsky 1957) for the following reasons. First, (208a-b) are well-formed only if *shi* is stressed (cf. (206b)), in which case the positive polarity of the predicate is emphatically contrasted with its negative polarity. For example, (208b) would be an appropriate negative response in contrast to the assertion "he's never been to Canada." This contrastiveness is clearly a feature associated with the CFM rather than with the copula. Secondly, the copula *shi* in Chinese functions as the main verb in a sentence and is usually grammatical obligatory (e. g. * *ta xuesheng* "he (is) a student"); while the CFM *shi* functions as a quasi-verb (Chapter 3), and is grammatically optional, as would be the case with (207), where the absence of *shi*... (*de*) would not affect grammaticality of the sentence. Since (208a-b) are still grammatical without *shi*, it must be a CFM rather than a copula.

Next, consider (209), where *shi* is not stressed:

(209) ta-de bizi shi hong de.
3s-GEN nose CPL red MM
"His nose is red."
他的鼻子是红的。

Structurally, *shi* in (209) occurs before an AP, a seeming violation of the pre-NP constraint and yet the sentence is still grammatical. However, we will argue that (209) actually has an underlying structure like (210):

(210)
```
                S
              /   \
         NP          VP
       /    \      /    \
    NP    N1   V        NP
    |     |    |      /    \
    |     |    |   AP  |    N2
    |     |    |    |  |    |
   tade bizi_i shi hong de  e_i
```
where the unrealized N_2 is coreferential with N_1. In support of this analysis is the fact that APs in Chinese behave like verbs (Chao 1968) and cannot occur independently after the copula without a following *de* (cf. (206b)):

(211) *tade bizi shi hong.

If the copula could indeed occur before an AP, we should expect (211) to be grammatical, which is in fact not the case. On the other hand, this unstressed *shi* cannot be a CFM, which should be stressed in pre-AP/VP positions (cf. (208)). As for *de*, it is recognized as a general-purpose modifier marker in Chinese (MM) (Ross, 1983), which may occur with or without a following head noun, especially when the latter is a noun with a general meaning such as "person" or "thing", or when its meaning is recoverable from the context, as is the case here. The obligatory cooccurrence of *de* with *shi* in (209), then, suggests that what underlyingly follows *de* is an unrealized head noun (i. e. "bizi"). Thus what looks like a copula + AP structure has in fact an underlying copula + NP structure. The constraint that the copula, like the demonstrative, occurs only before an NP is respected.

Synchronic evidence presented above shows that in modern Chinese, the copula *shi* is in general subject to the same constraint as the demonstrative *shi* (in Archaic Chinese), whereas the CFM *shi* is free of this constraint. Putting this in historical perspective, if we assume that the demonstrative use diachronically precedes other uses, there will be three logically possible routes of derivation:

(212) a. demonstrative > CFM > copula;

b. demonstrative > copula > CFM;

c. demonstrative > {copula, CFM}

where the braces {...} indicate simultaneous derivation of the copula and the CFM functions from the demonstrative.

The argument and evidence presented so far favours (212b), which conforms to Lightfoot's (1979) Transparency Principle, which "requires derivations to be minimally complex and initial, underlying structures to be 'close' to their respective surface structures" (p. 187) in order to preserve communicability between generations. New categories are created through reanalysis of grammatical constructions whereby exceptionality is grammaticalized and derivational complexity eliminated. In other words, changes in grammar may make the existing initial structure perceptually opaque to the language learner. Then reanalysis occurs and renders the initial structures more transparent to facilitate language acquisition. Such reanalysis often causes categorial change, among other things. For example, the development of English for-to infinitive can be shown to follow from the Transparency Principle (Lightfoot 1979: 188):

> in the early stage *for* occurs sometimes as a preposition (*I bought it for Mary, etc.*), sometimes as a COMP [(*for to go is necessary*)]; thus the *for* in the new construction of [*for us to go is necessary*] was of unclear category membership and could be analyzed as a preposition or as a COMP, causing potential confusion for the language learner. This indeterminacy was removed by the final change, whereby all *fors* were levelled and analyzed as prepositions.

Presumably, the Transparency Principle is also relevant in the present discussion on the development of Chinese *shi*. As will be shown in 6.3.2, at a certain stage in its development, *shi* was analyzable either as a demonstrative pronoun or as a copula, causing possible confusion in the language learner. The problem was later solved by reanalyzing *shi* as a copula.

Minimally complex derivation is also evident. In modern Chinese, intensifiers like *zhen* 真 ("really") and *dou/jie* 都/皆 ("all") obligatorily precede the copula *shi* 是 in equational sentences, but in Archaic Chinese, they occur after the pronoun *shi* 是. To wit

(213) a. Wang yue: "*shi* *zhen* wu shou fa zhi chen ye."
king say DEM really my abide law MM subject DP
"The king says: 'he is really a law-abiding subject of mine.'"
(*Han Fei Zi*: 3rd c. BC)
"王曰：'是真吾守法之臣也。'"《韩非子》

b. qi qiu shi wu yi. *Shi* *jie* qiu ming shi zhe ye.
PRON seek truth not PRT DEM all seek fame such person DP

"They are not seeking truth. They are all after fame as a matter of fact."
(*Zhuang Zi*: 4th c. BC)
"其求实无矣。是皆求名是者也。"《庄子》

The intensifiers *zhen* and *jie* follow the pronoun *shi* in (213a) and (213b), respectively. In modern Chinese, such adverbs precede the copula *shi*, or the CFM *shi*, as in (214).

(214) Zhen *shi* / **shi zhen* ta shuo de.
really CFM he say MM
"It is really he who said it."
真是 / ＊是真 他说的。

We may use this as a parameter and label it "pre-intensifier". Now recall the pre-NP constraint. Since demonstratives (DEM), copulas (CPL), and contrastive focus marker (CFM) can all occur in pre-NP position, to highligt their differences, we need to view the constraint conversely in terms of compatibility of the demonstrative, the copula or the CFM with a following non-NP. As a result, we have (215):

(215)

	DEM	CPL	CFM
pre-non-NP position	–	–	+
pre-intensifier position①	+	–	–

According to (215), the demonstrative *shi* 是 (in archaic use) differs from the CFM *shi* 是 by two structural properties but differs from the copula *shi* only by one. Since both (212a) and (212c) involve the change DEM > CFM, a more complex derivation than that represented by (212b), which involves only one feature-value change, by the minimal complexity condition of the Transparency Principle, (212b) would be the most plausible process of diachronic change. The closer diachronic relationship of the demonstrative to the copula than to the CFM, as suggested by (212b), is supported by the fact that the structural similarity between the demonstrative and the copula outweighs that between the demonstrative and the CFM,

① There is a crucial difference between these two constraints: grammatically, the non-NPs in the pre-non-NP constraint are complements or arguments (i. e. syntactic heads), whereas intensifiers are merely modifiers (i. e. non-heads). This difference disassociates the two constraints by disallowing any entailing relationship thereof. With respect to DEM, this means that its compatibility with a following intensifier is not contradictory to its incompatibility with a following non-NP.

as shown in (215).

6.3.2 Diachronic evidence

So far, we have mainly examined synchronic evidence in arguing for the process DEM > COPULA > CFM. In doing so we have assumed that the demonstrative use is older than the other two and suggested that the copula *shi* derived from the demonstrative *shi* historically. We will now examine diachronic evidence for this claim.

In Archaic Chinese, equational sentences normally did not have a copula (Wang 1984), as for example

(216) a. qi mu yue: "Kongzi xian ren ye."
his mother say Confucius wise man DP
"His mother says: 'Confucius (is) a wise man.'"
(*Zhan Guo Ce*, 5th c. BC)
"其母曰:'孔子贤人也。'"《战国策》

b. wu ba zhe, san wang zhi zui ren ye.
five hegemon person three king GEN criminal person DP
"The five hegemons are criminals before the three kings."
(*Mencius*: *Gao Zi Xia*, 4th c. BC)
"五霸者,三王之罪人也。"《左传》

The modern Chinese copula, *shi* 是, however, occurs regularly in equational sentences. In fact, this copula originated as a demonstrative in Archaic Chinese (Wang 1984; Graham 1967), which could be used as a deictic pronoun (217a), or a resumptive pronoun (217b):

(217) a. fan ***shi*** bu si, yi yi yan zai!
contrary this not think just it PRT INT
"Do not think contrary to this, that's it!"
(*Shi*:*Wei Feng*:*Mang*, 12-6th c. B.C.)
"反是不思,亦以焉哉!"《诗:卫风:氓》

b. zhi zhi wei zhi zhi, bu zhi wei bu zhi, ***shi*** zhi ye.
know it as know it not know as not know this know DP
"To show that you know when you do know and to show that you don't know when you don't, that is true knowledge." (*Analect*, 5th c. B.C.)
"知之为知之,不知为不知,是知也。"《论语》

Sentences like (217b) can be interpreted as having a topic-comment structure like (218), where the resumptive demonstrative *shi* which is anaphoric to the preceding clause is the subject of the next clause (S2) in an earlier stage of the language. The reason for such an analysis is that in the period of Archaic Chinese, equational sentences as a rule did not use a copula, as shown in (216), and that there was no sentence where *shi* functions unequivocally as a copula verb.

(218) [S1] [*shi* S2]
DEM
↓ ↓
TOPIC COMMENT

Then, at a later stage, the topic-comment construction without a copula in the earlier stage was *reinterpreted* as a subject-predicate construction "with the resumptive pronoun now being reanalyzed as a copula" (Li & Thompson 1975: 424). This process of grammaticalization of the topic can be shown as (219):

(219) Earlier Stage ➤ Later Stage
TOPIC-COMMENT ➤ SUBJECT - PREDICATE
S1 *shi* S2 S1 *shi* S2
DEM ➤ **CPL**

This process of reanalysis first occurred with the resumptive pronoun *shi*, and subsequently probably through grammaticalization extended the copula use to the deictic *shi*. By the late Han period (1st—2nd c. AD), the use of *shi* as a copula was firmly established and became productive①:

(220) a. "ci bai wu shi he deng?" da yue: "ci *shi* xiao er."
this white thing CPL what kind answer say this CPL small child

---

① The exact time for the demonstrative > copula change is not clear. However, sporadic examples indicating the beginning of such change are found in the works of as early as the 3rd century BC, a time when equational sentences regularly did not require a copula. Minimal-pair examples like

Chi he zhong ye ... cf. ci shi he zhong ye
this what kind DP this CPL what kind DP
"What kind (is) this?..." "What kind is this?" (*Han Fei Zi*: 3rd c. BC)

clearly suggests the copular status of *shi*. However, as such examples are very rare and sporadic, they do not reflect a regular copula function of *shi* in the works of that period.

"What is this white stuff?" Answer: "it's small child.'"
(Translation of the Buddha's saying in late Han, 25-220 A. D.)
"此白物是何等?"答曰:"此是小儿。"

b. yu *shi* suo jia furen zhi fu ye.
I CPL PRON marry woman GEN father DP
"I am the father of the woman given in marriage."
(*Lun Heng* by Wang Chong, 1st c. A. D.)
"余是所嫁妇人之父也。"王充:《论衡》

In all the sentences above, *shi* is unquestionably copular, in that it is impossible to interpret *shi* as a demonstrative pronoun. For example, in (220a), if *shi* were a demonstrative, we would have two adjacent demonstratives, *ci* and *shi*, which is quite redundant and implausible. The copular function of *shi* in (220b) is obvious for similar reasons, and especially so when we compare (220b), which requires a grammaticalized copula, with an almost identical sentence (220c) from an older text, where the copula does not appear:

(220) c. yu er suo jia furen zhi fu ye.
I you PRON marry woman GEN father DP
"I am the father of the woman you gave in marriage."
(*Zhuo Zhuan*, 6-7th c. BC; from Li & Thompson 1975)
"余尔所嫁妇人之父也。"《左传》

To sum up, the diachronic development of *shi* in Chinese shows a process of reanalysis whereby an original resumptive pronoun in the comment section of a topic-comment construction was reinterpreted as a copula in the predicate of a subject-predicate construction. Thus, the demonstrative > copula part of the hypothesized change in (212b) is vindicated.

Finally, we turn to the evidence in support of the suggested derivational process whereby the CFM *shi* derived from the copula *shi*. It is commonly believed that *shi* as a CFM made its first appearance in the popular verses of the Yuan Dynasty (1271-1368 AD), and by the Ming Dynasty (1368-1644) such uses had become very productive. A survey of Classical Chinese literature shows, however, that the use of *shi* as a CFM may be dated as far back as the Tang Dynasty (618-907 AD), when examples of the following kind can be found in the poetry of the period:

(221) ming hui bu gan bian, xin zhuan shi *shi* nan
fame return not dare argue heart turn really CFM difficult

"(I) dare not argue for my reputation, but it is indeed difficult to change my mind." (Meng Jiao, *Xi Ku*)

"名迴不敢辩,心转实是难。"《孟郊:惜苦》

In (221), *shi* appears before an AP in its emphatic use and functions as a CFM. Thus the CPL > CFM part of (211b) is also attested.

6.4 The Common Pragmatic Function

The synchronic and diachronic evidence examined so far suggests that some historical linkage between *shi* as the (now obsolete) demonstrative, as the copula, and as the CFM in Chinese can be established. As noted in 6.2, there are other languages where the CFM takes the same form as the copula and/or the demonstrative. This phenomenon begs the question from a functional point of view: is this recurrent formal identity between the different grammatical categories a mere coincidence, or is there any common functional ground that motivates such identity?

On the basis of the assumption that "the coding relation between structure and function in syntax *is non-arbitrary*" (Givón 1984: 33), and that "recurrent identity of form between different grammatical categories will always reflect some perceived similarity in communicative function" (Haiman 1985: 19), (222) is proposed as a functional account for the formal identity between the demonstrative, the copula, and the CFM:

(222) **The prototypical function of the demonstrative, viz. deixis and/or anaphor, is shared by the copula and the contrastive focus marker in diachronic change**, in the following manner:

Demonstrative: **deictic-anaphoric** > Copula: **anaphoric**
CFM: **focal deictic**

That demonstratives have a deictic function is self-evident: prototypically, by pointing to some person or entity, the speaker clearly identifies the referent in the discourse exophorically. As Sebeok (1994: 31) points out, a demonstrative is indexical insofar as "its signifier is continuous with its signified," spatially and temporally anchoring the referent in the discourse. As shown in 6.3.2, the demonstrative is also anaphoric, especially when it is used as a resumptive pronoun. In both cases, its function may be said to be one of indicative identification.

The anaphoric function of the copula is most evidently seen in languages in which the copula agrees with the subject in person, number, case, and/or gender. In other words, the fact that in these languages the copula recapitulates the nominal properties of the subject is a clear indication of anaphor. Even in languages without such overt AGR features, the copula still relates the predicate to the (usually preceding) subject, with anaphoric reference. Diachronically, when a demonstrative develops a copular function, it may lose its deictic power (as in the case of the Latin *ille*) but still retains its anaphoric function inasmuch as grammatical AGR is concerned (Mey 1993).

As for the CFM, the term CFM itself suggests a function of *contrastive* focus deixis. In languages like English, contrastive focus can be said to be marked both by the structural configuration and by the copula-like CFM (6.2). In languages like Chinese and Mopun that lack overt movement (Huang 1982), where the focused constituent is in the same position as in a corresponding non-cleft sentence, the CFM is the only means to deictically identify the contrastive focus.

In terms of information structure, however, since identification normally relates two *definite* entities, what is being focused upon by the CFM is usually "not new in the sense that it is completely out of consciousness. What is new is that [the element being focused] is the particular one which fits the description in [the clause which contains backgrounded information,] i. e. it is chosen as the correct object from a closed set of given possibilities and is therefore proclaimed as the correct element of such an exhaustive listing" (Brömser 1984: 329; Chafe 1974). Thus cleft sentences belong to the "special and readily identifiable class" (Chafe 1974: 118) "which express[es] a *contrast*" (Brömser 1984: 329) (italics mine). The CFM in such sentences helps to single out the element in contrastive focus in an unambiguous way, hence its focus identification function.

Given the respective functional domains of the demonstrative, the copula, and the CFM, we can see that if the original function(s) of an older category (i. e. DEM) is retained to a certain measure in more recently derived categories (i. e. CPL or CFM), the original isomorphemic relationship between form and meaning/function may be retained as well. As a result, the form may remain unchanged even if the functional domain of a newer category only partially overlaps those of the older one. In a word, it has been shown that the formal identity obtaining between the three categories is not a mere historical coincidence, but is motivated by their functional similarity.

6.5 Crosslinguistic Evidence

Having examined Chinese in some detail and proposed a functional account for the formal identity among the demonstrative, the copula and the CFM, we will now turn to some other languages to see if such cross-categorial formal identity occurs recurrently across languages. Five languages in addition to Chinese will be discussed: Hebrew, Margi, Mokilese, Kusaiean, and Malayalam.

6.5.1 Hebrew

In present tense equational sentences in Hebrew, a demonstrative *ze* or a personal pronoun *hu* is usually used to replace the otherwise used copula *h_y_y* (Berman 1978; Li & Thompson 1975). Thus in (223a), the use of *ze* mirrors the resumptive use of the Mandarin Chinese *shi* in (217b); likewise, the use of *hu* as a copula is seen in (223b-c):

(223) a. she-hu axrai lamaase (**ze**) barur lexulam
that-he responsible for-the-dead DEM clear to-all
"That he is responsible for the dead is clear to all."

b. ata (hu) ha-ganav
2s 3s/CPL the-thief
"You are the thief."

c. ani hu ha-student se-mose diber itxa alav
1s CPL the-student that-Moshe spoke with-you about-him
"I'm the student that Moshe told you about."

Li & Thompson (1975) relate *hu* to the Chinese *shi* by suggesting that it is being reanalyzed as a copula in Modern Hebrew. This is confirmed by several structural parallels:

1) Sentences like (223) can be uttered with an intonation suitable for a single, simple sentence, without a break after the subject, a feature that characterizes a subject-predicate structure.
2) The subject of a subject-predicate equational sentence can be indefinite, but the topic in a topic-comment sentence cannot.
3) *hu* can appear with a non-third person subject (e.g. (223b-c)), in which case *hu* cannot possibly have a 3rd person singular referent and has to be analyzed as a

copula.

As for *ze*, its copula function is more clearly seen in terms of agreement features. In declarative equational sentences, *ze* agrees in gender with the predicate NP if the latter is predicational. Consider (224) in casual Hebrew:

(224) ha-bayit shelha *zot* *dugma* *tova* (Glinert 1989:189)
the-house(m) your CPL(F) example good(F)
"Your house is a good example."

zot in (224) is the feminine inflection of *ze*, and agrees in gender with the feminine predicational NP *tova* rather than with the masculine subject NP *ha-bayit*. Given that deictic determiners generally follow the head noun in Hebrew, if *zot* were a true demonstrative, it would agree with the masculine subject NP and take the masculine form *ze*. The fact to the contrary casts doubt on *ze* as a demonstrative and suggests that *ze*, like *hu*, may have been reanalyzed as a copula, which, unlike *hu*, usually agrees with the predicate complement (Glinert 1989: 189,191). As to the somewhat idiosyncratic agreement of the copula with the predicate complement rather than the more common agreement with the subject, Haiman (1985), in examining similar data from Israeli Hebrew in terms of interplay between code and message, attributes it to a less ritualized grammatical (sub) system in which the speaker's message-based choice overrides the automatized code.

While Li & Thompson (1975) only mention the optionality of the pronoun-like forms in sentences like (223a) and (223b), Berman (1978: 207-208) points out that in a sentence like (223b), if *hu* does appear, "the effect achieved by having a 3rd-person pronoun 'copy' [= copula in Li & Thompson] following a non-3rd-person Subject is of a kind of 'clefting', with its concomitant emphasis manifested by the obligatory contrastive stress on the Subject pronoun." In other words, the presence of *hu* serves a contrastive focus marking function:

(225) a. **ata** *hu* haxashud
2s CPL the-suspect
"*You* are the suspect. / It is you who are the suspect."

b. **ani** *hu* she-pihakti (Glinert 1989)
1s CPL who I = yawned
"It is I who yawned."

The structural clefting with *hu* as the CFM is more clearly shown in (225b), which, by using a relative pronoun *she-*, shows a bi-clausal structure.

Like *hu*, *ze* can also be used as a CFM in cleft sentences to mark contrastive focus, and when thus used it precedes the focused constituent (Glinert: 422f):

(226) a. *ze* bney-adam tovim o bney-adam ra'im she-rotsim et ze?

CFM people good or people bad who-want OM it

"Is it good or bad people that want it?"

b. *ze* oti ra'it ba-shuk

CFM me you-saw in-the-market

"It is me you saw in the market."

c. *ze* ani she-pihakti

CFM 1s who-yawned

"It is I who yawned."

(226a) and (226b) show, respectively, that the focused constituent can be either the subject or the object in the clause. (226a) and (226c) show that the relative marker *she-* can head the presupposed clause.

In sum, Hebrew parallels Chinese in terms of both cross-categorial formal identity and diachronic relationship between the categories, though the exact path of derivation involving the CFM is less clear. The difference seems to be that while Chinese subsequently lost the pronominal function of *shi* following its reinterpretation as a copula, Hebrew nevertheless has retained the pronominal function for *ze/hu*.

6.5.2 Margi

In Margi, a Chadic language spoken in West Africa, the common demonstrative pronouns are *ku* "this", *ta* "that", etc. There also exists a morpheme *ŋu*, whose deictic use has now become largely obsolete and is found only in a few words, for example, *uven* "here" (probably from *u* "in" + *ivi* "place" + *ŋu* "this"). Apart from its deictic meaning, its structural properties also show that this morpheme was originally a demonstrative. Structurally, *ŋu* parallels *ku* in that (i) both can be used to nominalize adjectives, as in (227), and (ii) both can be used as a relative pronoun if the relativized NP is the subject in the relative clause, as in (228).

(227) kə/ŋə dəgal

DEM big

"the big one"

(228) a. naja ga kətər mdə *ku* at dəar dəl

3s saved man who fell-into-river

"He saved the man who fell into the river."

b. ... ular ja mji mətlu *ŋu* wudə mama

saw two people who brothers

"He saw two people who were brothers."

Margi does not use a copula in equational sentences normally, the predicate NP usually following the subject directly. But sometimes, either the third person singular pronoun *naja* or the demonstrative *ŋu* may occur between subject and predicate "as a quasi-copula" (Hoffmann 1963: 275):

(229) a. hya ku *naja* mala

dog this CPL bitch

"This dog is a bitch."

b. kəkə'yar ka*ŋu* mənagu

these CPL good

"These are good."

c. ja-*ŋ*

it CPL

"That's it!"

In (229c), where no expletive subject NP is required, only the predicate NP is obligatory, and the copula *ŋu* occurs at the end.

Like *shi* in Mandarin Chinese and *ze* in Modern Hebrew, the demonstrative pronoun *ŋu* in Margi has probably been reanalyzed as a copula. There are at least three pieces of evidence in support of this. Firstly, with nominal predicates, *ŋu* can follow plural NPs, as in

(230) nanda *ŋu*

3pl CPL

"It is they."

Given the existence of plural demonstratives *kuku'yr or kuku'yar ku* "these", and given that a demonstrative in Margi agrees in number with the noun it modifies, if what follows the NP in (230) were a true demonstrative, one of the plural demonstratives should have been used instead of the singular *ŋu*. The fact that what actually shows up is the latter suggests that this morpheme has probably lost most of its demonstrative function and been reanalyzed as a copula. Besides, it is rather unusual for a personal pronoun, which already has definite and complete reference, to be further designated by a demonstrative. Secondly, (230) would not be a sentence if *ŋu* were not a copula-like verb. Thirdly, *ŋu* is not mutually exclusive with the more common demonstrative *ku*. Consider (229b) again. Given that in general members of the same grammatical paradigm tend to be mutually exclusive with regard to a certain syntactic position, if *ŋu* were a genuine demonstrative, we would have two adjacent demonstratives with the same meaning and function, which is both structurally and pragmatically quite implausible, not to mention their disagreement with each other in number. On the other hand, if we analyze *ŋu* as a copula, there will be no such problems.

Hoffmann (1963: 89) also notes that, from the use of *ŋu* (as a copula) in nominal sentences is "derived the use of *ŋu* as a particle, introduced between subject and predicate, in order to give the subject a certain emphasis." In fact, a cleft reading is possible:

(231) a. ni *ŋu* samən
1s CFM brother
"*I* am your brother. / It is I who am your brother."

b. ni -ŋ atsianyi
1s CFM kill-him
"*I* killed him. / It is I who killed him."

Such emphatic use of *ŋu* corresponds to the CFM use of *ze/*hu in Hebrew (cf. (225-226)). In addition, the whole nominal predication in (229c), *ja-ŋ*, in which *ŋu* is used as a copula, may also be used as a CFM. For instance,

(232) kər banban *jaŋ* attəny
headache CFM hurt-him
"*Headache* hurts him. / It is headache that hurts him."

(232) provides us with a clue in favour of the possible route of diachronic change DEM > CPL > CFM. Making the reasonable assumption based on the non-use of a copula in general that the now obsolete demonstrative use precedes the copula and CFM uses historically, if the ordering were DEM > CFM > CPL, then we would expect the CFM form in (232) to be *ŋu*, a direct derivation from the demonstrative form, rather than *jaŋ*, a form in which *ŋu* is used as a copula. The fact to the contrary suggests that CFM use must have derived from the copula use, at which stage *ŋu* is suffixed to *ja*, and that only at a later stage did the whole fused form begin to be used as CFM. Therefore, the diachronic change is more likely to be DEM > CPL > CFM in Margi, just as in Chinese.

6.5.3 Mokilese

In Mokilese, a Micronesian language with a basic SVO order, any major constituent, including the VP, can be cleft focused by being preposed to the sentence initial position, with the remainder of the sentence treated as a relative clause headed by the relative marker *ma* (Harrison 1976):

(233) a. ngoah wahdo mwingehu
1s bought food
"I bought the food."

b. ngoah ma wahdo mwingehu
1s RM bought food
"It was I who bought the food."

Parallel to this cleft construction is an alternative cleft pattern (234), where the initial cleft focus is preceded by *ioar* which functions as a CFM:

(234) a. *ioar* woall-o ma wia mehu (Harrison 1976)
CFM man-that RM did that
"It was that man who did it."

b. *ioar* kida ma ngoah nimen dupukda
CFM guitar RM I want buy
"It's a guitar that I want to buy."

According to Harrison (1976: 309), *ioar* is probably "the last survivor of a set of 'pointing determiners,'" i. e. deictic pronouns which have become obsolete. In fact, this last survivor is so rare that evidence of its synchronic demonstrative use is lacking from the available Mokilese data *per se*. However, its cognates *iet*, *ien*, and *io* in Ponapean, another language in the same Ponapeic subgroup of the Micronesian languages, are still being used as demonstratives (Harrison 1976), and are glossed as such in the list of cognates between Kusaiean and Ponapean provided by Lee (1975), where *io* (spelled as *o*) and *ien* are presented as cognates to the Kusaiean demonstratives *ah* and *an*, respectively.

What Harrison (1976) failed to observe is the morphological structure of *ioar*, which, when compared with a synchronically productive DEM paradigm in Mokilese, provides clues to its diachrony. The paradigm, together with their cognates in Ponapean and Kusaiean, is shown in Table 6.1:

Table 6. 1 ***Demonstrative cognates in Mokilese, Ponapean and Kusaiean***

	Mokilese	Ponapean	Kusaiean
"this"	-e / -i	iet	ah
"that"	-en / -n	ien	an
"thither"	-o / -u	io	?

The Mokilese paradigm in Table 6. 1 shows two variants for the DEM "this": *-e* and *-i*. It is contended here that *ioar* actually derived from the second variant diachronically, based on morphophonemic similarity between the two morphemes. This similarity becomes more transparent if we, by assuming a bimorphemic structure for *ioar*, analyze it as composed of *i-* "this" and some other morpheme. This analysis is supported by the existence of a delimiting suffix *-oar* in Mokilese, glossed as "only" and suffixed directly to a NP or determiner such as a demonstrative. It is this delimiting suffix, I suggest, that constitutes the latter part of *ioar*, i. e. *ioar* may well be analyzed as *i-oar* "this-only". Given its use as a CFM, which identifies as contrastive focus a constituent in a sentence whose reference tends to be exclusive in the given discourse, this analysis is quite plausible both semantically and pragmatically. In short, the Mokilese CFM *ioar* can be analyzed as incorporating a demonstrative whose use has become largely obsolete probably as a result of the incorporation.

In addition to its (obsolete) demonstrative use, *ioar* is sometimes found to also function as a copula in equational sentences with definite predicate NPs. In general, an equational sentence may be either predicational or identificational, depending on whether the predicate NP is indefinite or definite. Mokilese identificational equational sentences allow for a copula. Compare

(236) a. John johnpadahkmen
John teacher
"John is a teacher."

b. minpas-e *ioar* noai pinjel-wa
one-this CPL my pencil-DET
"This one is my pencil."

c. me *ioar* woal-wa ma wia mehu
this CPL man-the RM did that

"This is the man who did it."

The predicate NP in (236a) is predicational by virtue of being indefinite, and *ioar* is not used. The predicate NPs in (236b-c), on the other hand, are both definite referential NPs; and between the subject and the predicate appears *ioar*, whose function is clearly that of a copula. Furthermore, its copular status is vindicated by the same argument as presented in the Margi case with regard to the property of mutual exclusiveness between members of the same grammatical paradigm. More specifically, if *ioar* in (236b) or (236c) were analyzed as a demonstrative, there would coexist two adjacent demonstratives for no obvious reasons at all, which renders the analysis implausible. The copula analysis, as in the Margi case, eliminates such problems. Thus, polysemous relationship obtains between *ioar* as CFM, as DEM, and as CPL depending on the syntactic position in which it occurs in a sentence.

There is no direct evidence for diachronic relationships between the three categories in Mokilese. However, if we assume that where polysemy exists between a form and two or more related functions the obsolete function tends to diachronically precede the synchronically active ones, then the obsoleteness of *ioar* as DEM may suggest its diachronic precedence to the other two functions. Moreover, we notice in (234) that when *ioar* is used as a CFM, it occurs to the left of the focused constituent, contrary to our usual expectation of a VO language. On the other hand, the demonstrative *ioar*, by analogy to other currently operative demonstratives, and the copula *ioar*, occur in positions predictable for a VO language. This may well reflect an on-going word order change in Mokilese, and the CFM function of *ioar* is probably a more recent innovation than the CPL function, not to say the DEM function. Thus, the diachronic development of the functions of *ioar* can be reasonably shown as DEM > CPL > CFM①, which mirrors that in Chinese.

6.5.4 Kusaiean

Kusaiean, another Micronesian language with a basic SVO order, presents a somewhat different picture. In Kusaiean, the cleft focus occurs in sentence-initial position, followed immediately by *pa*; and the whole sentence must end with the particle *ah or uh* (Lee 1975):

---

① However, semantic considerations based on the above analysis of the morphological makeup of *ioar* seem to favour the precedence of CFM to CPL.

(237) wes se **pa** nga enenuh **uh**
shirt this CPL 1s need PRT
"It is the shirt that I need."

Two things are worth noting in (237). First, *pa* is glossed as CPL, as can be seen from its occurrence in identificational equational sentences. As in Mokilese and some other languages, Kusaiean identificational equational sentences differ structurally from their predicational counterparts in having a copula, *pa*, between the subject NP and the predicate NP:

(238) a. nga tuhlihk lutlut se
1s student one
"I am a student."

b. mwet sac *pa* mwet pihsrapasrsac
man that CPL thief that
"That man is the thief."

The predicate NP in (238a) is predicational by virtue of being indefinite, and no copula is used. In contrast, (238b) is identificational with a definite predicate NP, and *pa* is present, which functions as a copula. This same form is used in cleft sentences and occurs adjacent to the cleft focus, posing as a candidate for the CFM.

Interestingly, the sentence-final particle *ah* or *uh* occurs *obligatorily* in sentences like (237), and poses as another potential CFM. This *ah/uh* is in fact a demonstrative, which use is self-evident from such examples as *ik uh* "these fish" and *infacl ah* "in this river". As for the relationship between *pa* and *ah/uh*, there is yet no evidence suggesting their diachronic relatedness. Therefore, the two grammatical categories, copula and demonstrative, are realized by two different morphemes in Kusaiean.

Given that a Kusaiean cleft sentence requires both a copula-like form and a demonstrative pronoun and either can be a candidate for the CFM, which of the two actually serves as the CFM? Considering the close linguistic distance between the focus marker and the focused constituent observed in many languages (e. g. Breton, in Timm 1987), it would seem more likely that the copula-like form serves the function of the CFM, which is in part supported by Lee's (1976) glossing of *pa* as "focus marker". However, the obligatory presence of the demonstrative in cleft sentences still remains to be accounted for. It is suggested here that both serve to mark contrastive focus but at different levels, i. e. the sentence-final demonstrative/

particle marks, on a more general level, the whole sentence as contrastively focusing on one of its constituents, whereas the copula marks a specific constituent as the contrastive focus *per se*. Otherwise, it would seem rather implausible for *ah/uh*, obligatory as it is, to mark a distant focus. If this analysis is uncontested, we would have a cleft structure like (239), in which the copula and the demonstrative pronoun, albeit lack of evidence for their diachronic relationship, jointly mark a cleft sentence but each operates at a different level.

(239)

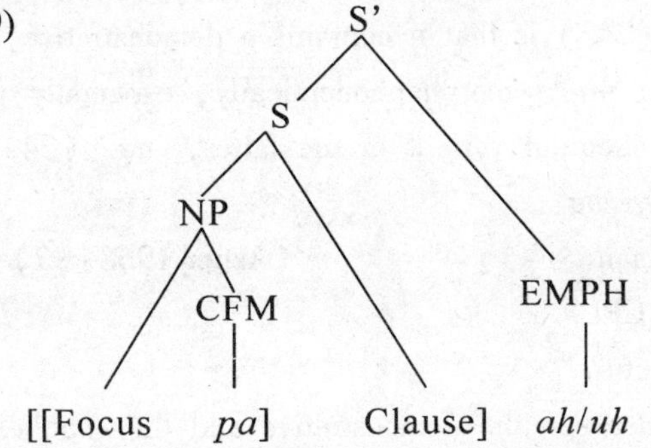

6.5.5 Malayalam

Finally, Malayalam, a Dravidian language with a basic SOV order, presents further evidence showing the formal identity of the three categories in question.

In Malayalam, the copula used in equational nominal sentences is *aanə*, with two variant forms: *aakunu*, used in formal, written style, and *-aa*, in informal colloquial use (Asher 1968: 95). Examples of *aanə* as copula in equational sentences follow:

(240) avan joon aanə (Asher 1968: 96)
3s John CPL
"He is John."

(241) kutti penn-aanə
child girl-CPL
"The child is a girl."

This copula is also used in predicational copula sentences where the predicative codes adjectival meaning, which is usually expressed, as a typological feature of Malayalam, through abstract nouns or "adjective" modifiers of the head noun within a predicative NP. For example, the adjectival meaning of the predicative is expressed through an abstract noun, *nissabdam* "silence" in (242), and as an adjective modifier plus a generic noun, *pazayat* "something old", in (243).

(242) viitu nissabdam -aanə
house silence CPL
"The house is silent."

(243) aa kettitam pazayat -aanə
that building something = old CPL
"That building is old."

What is more interesting about (243) is that it contains a demonstrative, *aa*, which formally resembles the copula *-aanə* morphophonemically, especially when compared with the aforementioned colloquial variant of the latter, *-aa*. (244) is another example with the demonstrative *aa*:

(244) *aa* tootti cutalamuttu -aanə (Asher 1968: 97)
that scavenger Chudalamuttu CPL
"That scavenger is Chudalamuttu."

Apart from the formal identity between the demonstrative and the copula, the same form can also be found in its use as a CFM. In what Asher (1968) calls an "emphatic" construction, *-aanə* is added to some other word in the sentence, accompanied by the nominalization of the finite verb (through the addition of the neuter nominal suffix *-atə*), "to give emphasis to that part of the sentence to which *-aanə* is attached" (p. 107). Consider the following examples:

(245) a. ñaan atu kantu
1s it saw
"I saw it."

b. ñaan-*aanə* atu kant-atə
1s CFM it saw NOM
"It was I who saw it."

(246) a. aval aare annane vilikkunnu
she whom like-that is-calling
"Whom is she calling like that?"

b. aval aare-*yaanə* annane vilikkunn-atə
she whom CFM like-that is-calling-NOM
"Whom is it that she is calling like that?"

(247) a. atəennilninnə avan pratiiksikkunnu
it me = from 3s expect

"He expects it from me."

b. atəennilninn-*aanə* avan pratiiksikkunn-atə
it me = from CFM he expect NOM
"It is from me that he expects it."

In (245-247), what minimally distinguishes a cleft sentence from a non-cleft is the CFM *-aanə*, plus the accompanying nominalizer, a pattern not unlike that in Chinese. Thus, we find that in Malayalam, the demonstrative, the copula, and the CFM all share the form *-aa(nə)*. Although the exact path of diachronic change from one category to another cannot be ascertained at this point due to paucity of data, it *can* be established that the same kind of formal identity between the categories obtains in Malayalam as in the other languages that have been examined.

6.6 An Iconic Account

Table 6.2 summarizes the crosslinguistic formal identity obtaining recurrently between the three grammatical categories.

Table 6.2 ***Recurrent formal identity between the CFM, the copula and the Demonstrative in six languages***

	Chinese	Hebrew	Margi	Mokilese	Kusaiean	Malayalam
CFM	*shi*	*ze/(hu)*	*ŋ u*	*ioar*	*pa... ah/uh*	*-aan ə*
Copula	*shi*	*ze/(hu)*	*ŋ u*	*ioar*	*pa*	*aa(nə)*
Demonstrative	*shi*	*ze/(hu)*	*ŋ u*	*io*	*ah/uh*	*aa*

Now turning back to (204), we have seen that both diachronic relatedness (204b) and functional commonality (204c) are responsible for the recurrent formal identity between the different grammatical categories. On the one hand, these languages, again with the exception of Kusaiean and possibly of Malayalam, manifest to different extent diachronic relationships between the three grammatical categories. On the other hand, we can perceive a pragmatic function of *deixis/anaphor* underlying these categories in all the languages, each with its sub-functional domain. It is this underlying function, it is contended, that historically motivated the formal identity between the copula, the CFM and the demonstrative pronoun in languages that exhibit such identity. The function proposed is a kind of meta-function whose underspecification helps unify the sub-functions, each represented by a different grammatical category. The whole process can be perceived as a linguistic form shifting its sub-functional domains within a general functional domain while keeping its formal integrity. We can envisage a function hierarchy whose relationship to the same cross-categorial form can be diagrammed as Figure 6. 1, where F stands for the meta-function, C_n refers to grammatical categories realizing interrelated, specific functions (f_n), and X_i represents the recurrent identical form. Synchronically, the relationship of X_i to f_n is one of polysemy (i. e. related functions mapped onto the same form), which, from a semiotic point of view, is motivated by paradigmatic economy that economizes on the inventory of signs within a system. However, when we relate the form (X_i) to the generalized meta-function, the relationship of X_i to F at a higher level may be perceived as one of isomorphism. Therefore, the issue seems to boil down to the underlying isomorphemic principle of one form for one function/meaning (Haiman 1985), which, by manifesting itself at a more abstract level, motivates the phenomenon in question.

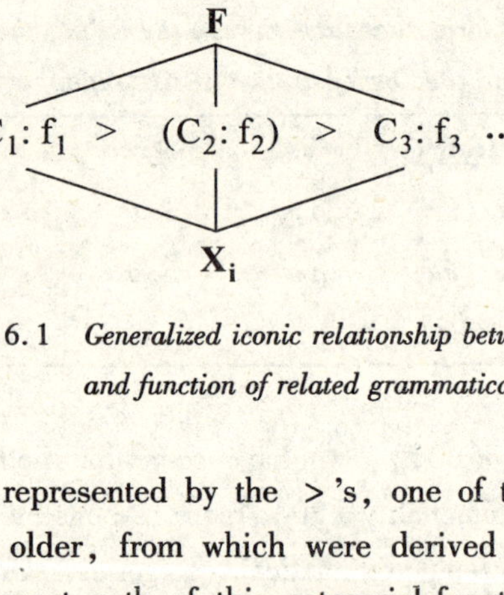

Figure 6. 1 *Generalized iconic relationship between form and function of related grammatical categories*

Diachronically, as represented by the >'s, one of the grammatical categories (e. g. DEM) may be older, from which were derived the other categories with related functions. The exact path of this categorial-functional shift is a language-specific matter; for example, some languages may choose not to have a copula, and such optionality is represented in Figure 6. 1 by the brackets. Likewise, given that the categories may coexist in a language synchronically, as most of the languages examined have shown, a category (e. g. DEM) may share a sub-function with another category (e. g. CPL) at one stage, and another sub-function with a different category (e. g. CFM) at another stage. As a result, although all the categories involved are related in one way or another to the meta-function, they may not necessarily all share exactly the same sub-functions synchronically (e. g. CPL and CFM).

6.7 Conclusion

In conclusion, linguistic change in morpho-syntax can involve inter-categorial transfer of the same form, often reflected synchronically through formal identity among coexisting categories. Such transfer can be motivated and conditioned by semantico-functional similarity between the categories involved, as manifested in the formal identity between the CFM, the demonstrative and/or the copula in many languages. Evidence for this theoretical tenet has been obtained in this chapter through analysis of six languages: Chinese, Hebrew, Margi, Mokilese, Kusaiean, and Malayalam, where the three categories are shown to be by and large diachronically related, which in turn is motivated by their sharing of the meta-function of deixis-anaphor.

Therefore, deixis-anaphor serves as the pragmatic-functional basis for function-internal evolution involving inter-categorial transfer of the same form. Furthermore, as deixis-anaphor is a meta-function and the functions of CPL and CFM are its sub-domains, the relationship between the linguistic form and the meta-function is in fact isomorphimic at a general level, though at a more specific level the polysemous relationship is motivated by paradigmatic economy. Thus viewd, polysemy among DEM, CPL and CFM may be said to be motivated by both iconicity and economy.

Chapter 7 Conclusion

This book has investigated crosslinguistic cleftability of different grammatical functions and categorial types to further studies on the Accessibility Hierarchy and on clefting. Inspired initially by Keenan and Comrie's Accessibility Hierarchy with respect to relativization, and following a systematic functional-typological approach, the author has advanced and examined three theories to account for cleftability in various languages, viz. the Cleftability Hierarchy, the Nouniness Principle, and the Thematicity Principle, all of which may be considered constraints on the patterns of variation in possible human languages in terms of cleftability.

The Cleftability Hierarchy, which is patterned after the Accessibility Hierarchy, as a potential universal accounts for cleftability of various NP functions by virtue of specifying a relative order of these functions in relation to cleftability. Methodologically, however, prior studies on the Accessibility Hierarchy did not adequately operationalize relative accessibility between the NP positions on the Hierarchy. For example, use of the grammaticality and/or the clefting strategy criteria without considering the distribution factor may overlook some subtle yet important differences in accessibility between the grammatical positions and subsequently result in an incomplete characterization of accessibility. Therefore, one of the main contributions of this book is to have developed a set of criteria to more fully operationalize cleftability in terms of grammaticality, the clefting strategy, distribution, frequency of occurrence, promotion, and precedence in language change. Such an enriched set of criteria make the proposed Cleftability Hierarchy more verifiable by being able to measure cleftability more sufficiently. In fact, crosslinguistic evidence has supported the Cleftability Hierarchy in all the above-mentioned parameters, which in turn lends further support to the Accessibility Hierarchy. As for the apparent counterevidence examined in the book, rather than invalidating the Cleftability Hierarchy, it shows the complex nature of the workings of the Cleftability Hierarchy, in the sense that some positions on the Hierarchy are subject to reinterpretation depending on typological parameters, or that the workings of the Hierarchy may interact with, and be negatively affected by, language specific constraints. In a word, results show that the Cleftability Hierarchy has considerable validity as far as NP positions are concerned.

On the other hand, it has also been shown that the Cleftability Hierarchy in its original form can not account for non-NP cleftability, especially when non-NPs become more cleftable in context. Given this context-sensitive nature of non-NP cleftability, even an extended Cleftability Hierarchy like (122) would not capture all the facts about non-NP cleftability. Therefore, a Nouniness Principle is proposed to supplement the Cleftability Hierarchy.

Dealing largely with semantic information, the Nouniness Principle supplements the Cleftability Hierarchy by virtue of its ability to account for context-dependent non-NP cleftability through the notion of *specificity*, expressed through restrictive modifiers, contrastiveness and nominal properties. Results from the investigation on non-NP clefting show a clear relationship between increased cleftability and increased nouniness as defined above, suggesting that the Nouniness Principle is a plausible account for non-NP cleftability both descriptively and in a way explanatorily. Moreover, the Nouniness Principle also works in conjunction with clefting strategies (17b) and distribution (17c), in that where both are at work, non-NP cleftability is greatest.

Despite the complementary nature of the Cleftability Hierarchy and the Nouniness Principle, they still leave some areas of cleftability unaccounted for, such as the relatively high cleftability of proposition-internal adjuncts, especially those of time and place, both inter-categorially and intracategorially. To deal with such limitations and to provide a more descriptive, more explanatory and unified account of cleftability, the Thematicity Principle is advanced which supersedes the Cleftability Hierarchy and the Nouniness Principle in the following ways:

(i) NPs are in general more thematic, and therefore more cleftable than APs, ADVPs and VPs; however, when the latter become more noun-like in context through increased specificity, their thematic potential is also increased and so is their cleftability.

(ii) Given the pragmatic function of cleft sentences, the order on the Cleftability Hierarchy can be predicted by the order on the Thematicity Scale. Thus, a more thematic NP position, e. g. SU, will be more cleftable.

(iii) Proposition-internal adjuncts of time and place are prototypical themes and have high thematic potential; hence they are highly cleftable.

An overview of the three theories, as has been shown, inevitably involves a comparison in terms of their adequacies of description and explanation. In the formal-generative framework, an explanation generally involves postulation of abstract structures or principles to account for surface structures, without reference to external factors such as semantico-pragmatic functions. In the functional-typological framework, an explanation involves external factors such as the "natural explanatory parameters" in terms of propositional content, discourse pragmatics, the processor, cognitive structure, world view pragmatics, etc. (Givón 1979) A formal model of abstract rules, in this view, is not an explanation, but simply a higher order of formalized description.

While both the formal-generative model and Givón's functional-typological model view description and explanation as dichotomous, Greenberg (1968, 1969) and Croft (1990), observing that in fact both models involve abstraction and external factors, treat description and explanation as scalar on a continuum of generality. According to this scalar model (Croft 1990: 248),

> a more general linguistic statement can be said to explain a more specific one, though it may itself be explained by a yet more general statement... [thus] any given statement is an explanation for a lower-level generalization, but a description in comparison to a higher level generalization.

The scalar model as suggested by Greenberg and Croft enables us to state the concluding remarks as follows. Cleftability is most adequately accounted for context-sensitively using structural *and* semantico-pragmatic information. While the AH-related Cleftability Hierarchy and the Nouniness Principle only partially fulfil such a task, the Thematicity Principle makes the most general statement about cleftability and therefore is the most plausible theory of cleftability as yet with most descriptive and explanatory adequacy.

In terms of future orientations of cleftability study, it should be pointed out firstly that the research reported in this book is predominantly qualitative, aiming at developing a plausible theory of cleftability. In that regard, the objective has been achieved. Future studies of more quantitative nature are needed to further validate the research findings. Secondly, in addition to the six criteria proposed in (17), the Cleftability Hierarchy may also be attested in terms of language acquisition, either longitudinally or cross-sectionally, and either in first language or in second language. Lastly, given the very low frequency of occurrence attested for some of the elements on the Thematicity Scale (e. g. DO, IO, OBL), future studies are expected to examine texts of other genres to determine if, and why, the same low frequency is recurrent.

All in all, through broader and more rigid operationalization and careful consideration of clefting and cleftability in context and in larger domains which involve both NPs and non-NPs, it has been established that a functional-typological theory based on structural and semantico-pragmatic constraints provides a natural and unified account of cleftability in language.

References

Akmajian, A. 1970. On deriving cleft-sentences from pseudo-cleft sentences. *Linguistic Inquiry* 1(2): 149-168.

Akmajian, A. 1979. *Aspects of the Grammar of Focus in English*. New York: Garland.

Allerton, D. J. 1978. The notion of "givenness" and its relations to presupposition and to theme. *Lingua* 44: 133-168.

Allan, K. 1987. Hierarchies and the choice of left conjuncts. *Journal of Linguistics* 23(1): 51-77.

Anderson, S. R. 1976. On the notion of subject in ergative languages. In C. Li (ed.), *Subject and Topic*, 1-63. New York: Academic Press.

Andrew, C. M. 1977. An experiment on focus. In M. Paradis (ed.). *The Fourth LACUS Forum*, 576-583. Columbia, SC: Hornbean.

Andrews, A. 1985. The major functions of the noun phrase. In T. Shopen (ed.), *Language Typology and Syntactic Description*, Vol. 1, 62-154. Cambridge: CUP.

Ariel, M. 1988. Referring and accessibility. *Journal of Linguistics* 24(1): 65-87.

Asher, R. E. 1968. Existential, possessive, locative and copulative sentences in Malayalam. In J. Verhaar (ed.), *The Verb "Be" and its Synonyms*, Vol. 6, 88-111. Dordrecht: D. Reidel.

Atlas, J. D. & Levinson, S. C. 1981. It-clefts, informativeness, and logical form: radical pragmatics (revised standard version). In P. Cole (ed.), *Radical Pragmatics*, 1-61. New York: Academic Press.

Awobuluyi, O. 1978. Focus construction as noun phrases. *Linguistic Analysis* 4: 93-114.

Bamgbose, A. 1966. *A Grammar of Yoruba*. Cambridge: CUP.

Barnstead, J. A. 1984. Ambiguities in the universal noun phrase accessibility hierarchy: the Ukrainian evidence. *Studia Ukrainica* 2: 145-154.

Barry, R. 1975. Topic in Chinese: an overlap of meaning, grammar and discourse function. In R. E. Grossman, L. J. San, & T. J. Vance (eds.), *CLS Papers from the Parasession on Functionalism*. Chicago: CLS.

Bennett, P. A. 1979. Observations on the transparency principle. *Linguistics* 17: 843-861.

Berman, R. A. 1978. *Modern Hebrew Structure*. Tel-Aviv: University Publishing Projects, Ltd.

Bolinger, D. 1972. A look at equations and cleft sentences. In E. S. Firchow et al. (eds.), *Studies for Einar Haugen*, 96-114. The Hague: Mouton.

Bolinger, D. 1977. *The Form of Language*. London: Longman.

Brennan, P. 1993. Custom builder falls in love with "pocket of wilderness". In *The Toronto Star*, May 1, 1993, E1.

Bresnan, J. (ed.) 1982. *The Mental Representation of Grammatical Relations*. Cambridge, Mass.: MIT Press.

Bresnan, J. & Grimshaw, J. 1978. The syntax of free relatives in English. *Linguistic Inquiry* 9: 331-391.

Brody, J. 1984. Cleft in Tojolabal Maya: structure and discourse function. *Journal of Mayan Linguistics* 4(2): 65-90.

Brömser, B. 1984. Towards a functional description of cleft constructions. *Lingua* 62: 325-348.

Bybee, J. 1985. Diagrammatic iconicity in stem-inflection relations. In J. Haiman (1985b).

Calude, A. 2008. Clefting and Extraposition in English. *ICAME Journal* 32: 7-33.

Chafe, W. L. 1974. Language and consciousness. *Language* 50: 111-133.

Chafe, W. L. 1976. Givenness, contrastiveness, definiteness, subjects, topics, and point of view. In C. Li (ed.), *Subject and Topic*, 25-56. New York: Academic Press.

Chao, Y-R. 1968. *A Grammar of Spoken Chinese*. Berkeley: University of California Press.

Charezinska, A. 1987. Radical pragmatics and the scope of negation. *Studia Anglica Posnaniensia* 29: 123-128.

Chen, J. 1984. *Hanyu Kouyu* (Spoken Chinese). Beijing: Beijing Press.

Chomsky, N. 1970. Remarks on nominalization. In R. Jacobs & P. Rosenbaum (*eds.*), *Readings in English Transformational Grammar*, 184-221. Waltham, Mass.: Ginn.

Chomsky, N. 1977. On wh-movement. In P. W. Culicover, T. Wasow & A. Akmajian (eds.), *Formal Syntax.* New York: Academic Press.

Chomsky, N. 1981. *Lectures on Government and Binding*. Dordrecht: Foris.

Chung, S. 1978. *Case Marking and Grammatical Relations in Polynesian.* Austin: University of Texas Press.

Clarke, H. H. & Haviland, S. E. 1977. Comprehension and the given-new contrast. In R. Freedle (ed.) *Discourse Production and Comprehension*, 1-40. Hillside, NJ: Erlbaum.

Cole, P. 1981. *Radical Pragmatics*. New York: Academic Press.

Cole, P. et al. 1977. Noun phrase accessibility and island constraints. In P. Cole & J. M. Sadock (eds.), *Syntax and Semantics*, Vol. 8, 27-46. New York: Academic Press.

Collins, P. C. 1987. Cleft and pseudo-cleft constructions in English spoken and written discourse. *ICAME Journal* 11: 5-17.

Collins, P. C. 1991. *Cleft and Pseudo-Cleft Constructions in English.* London: Routledge.

Collins, P. C. 2006. *It*-clefts and *wh*-clefts: prosody and pragmatics. *Journal of Pragmatics* 38: 1706-1720.

Comrie, B. 1981. *Language Universals and Linguistic Typology.* Chicago: University of Chicago Press.

Comrie, B. 1988. Passive and voice. In M. Shibatani (ed.), *Passive and Voice*, 9-24. Amsterdam: John Benjamins.

Contreras, H. 1976. *A Theory of Word Order with Special Reference to Spanish.* Amsterdam: North-Holland.

Cowell, M. W. 1964. *A Reference Grammar of Syrian Arabic.* Washington D. C.: Georgetown University Press.

Cozier, F. K. 2006. The co-occurrence of predicate clefting and wh-questions in Trinidad dialectal English. *Natural Language & Linguistic Theory* 24:655-688.

Craig, C. G. 1977. *The Structure of Jacaltec*. Austin: University of Texas Press.

Croft, W. 1990. *Typology and Universals*. Cambridge: CUP.

Dahl, Ö (ed.). 1974. *Topic and Comment, Contextual Boundness and Focus.* Helmu: bei den Autoren.

Dahlstrom, A. 1993. The syntax of discourse functions in Fox. In D. Peterson (ed.), *Proceedings of the 19th Annual Meeting of the Berkeley Linguistic Society*, 11-21. Berkeley: Berkeley Linguistic Society.

Declerck, R. 1983. Predicational clefts. *Lingua* 61: 9-45.

Declerck, R. 1984a. The pragmatics of It-clefts and WH-clefts. *Lingua* 64(4): 251-289.

Declerck, R. 1984. Some restrictions on clefts that highlight predicate nominals. *Journal of Linguistics* 20: 131-154.

Declerck, R. 1988. *Studies on Copular Sentences, Clefts and Pseudo-clefts*. Leuven: Leuven University Press.

De Groot, C. 1981. On *Theme* in functional grammar. In Hoekstra et al. (eds.), 1981, 75-88.

Delahunty, G. P. 1984. The analysis of English cleft sentences. *Linguistic Analysis* 13(2): 63-113.

Delin, J. & Oberlander, J. 1995. Syntactic constraints on discourse structure: the case of it-clefts. *Linguistics: An Interdisciplinary Journal of the Language Sciences*, 33(3): 465-500.

Devitt, D. 1990. The diachronic development of semantics in copulas. In K. Hall, J. Koenig, M. Meacham, S. Reinman & L. Sutton (eds.), *Proceedings of the 16th Annual Meeting of the Berkeley Linguistic Society*, 103-115. Berkeley: Berkeley Linguistic Society.

Dik, S. C. 1978. *Functional Grammar*. Amsterdam: North-Holland Publishing Co.

Dik, S. C. 1980. *Studies in Functional Grammar*. London: Academic Press.

Dik, S. C. 1985. Cleft and pseudo-cleft in functional grammar. In W. Zonneveld & F. Weerman (eds.), *Linguistics in the Netherlands* 1977-1979, 26-43. Dordrecht: Foris.

Dixon, R. 1979. Ergativity. *Language* 55: 59-138.

Doron, E. 1986. The pronominal "copula" as agreement clitic. In H. Borer (ed.), *Syntax and Semantics*, Vol. 19., 313-332. Orlando: Academic Press.

Dragunov, A. A. 1958. *Grammatical Studies of Modern Chinese*. Beijing: Kexue Chuban She.

Dryer, M. 1980. The positional tendencies of sentential noun phrases in universal grammar. *Canadian Journal of Linguistics* 25: 123-195.

Dyen, I. 1964. *Beginning Indonesian*. Office of Education, U. S. Department of

Health, Education, adn Welfare.

Eckman, F. 1988. Universals, typologies and interlanguage. In W. Rutherford (ed.), *Second Language Acquisition and Language Universals*. Amsterdam: John Benjamins.

Edmondson, J. A. 1977. Ergative language, accessibility hierarchies governing reflexive and questions of formal analysis. In W. Abraham (ed.), *Valence, Semantic Case, and Grammatical Relations*, 633-660. Amsterdam: Benjamins.

Eid, M. 1983. The copula function of pronouns. *Lingua* 59(1): 197-207.

Elbert, S. H. & Monberg, T. 1965. *From the Two Canoes*. Honolulu: University of Hawaii Press.

Ellis, J. & Boadi, L. 1969. "To be" in Twi. In J. W. M. Verhaar (ed.), *The Verb "Be" and Its Synonyms*, Vol. 9, 1-71. Dordrecht: D. Deidel Publishing Co.

Emonds, J. E. 1976. *A Transformational Approach to English Syntax*. New York: Academic Press.

Ennaji, M. & Sadiqi, F. 1986. The syntax of cleft sentence in Berber. *Studies in Language* 10(1): 53-77.

Escure, G. 1985. The Belizean copula: a case of semantic shift. In M. Dascal (ed.), *Dialogue: an Interdisciplinary Approach*, 265-279. Amsterdam: John Benjamins.

Feng, Li. 1993. The copula in Classical Chinese declarative sentences. *Journal of Chinese Linguistics* 21: 277-311.

Fichtner, E. 1993. Cleft sentences in English: a comprehensive view. *Word* 44 (1): 1-30.

Firbas, J. 1964. On defining the theme in functional sentence perspective. *Travaux Linguisticques de Prague* 1: 267-280.

Fletcher, P. 1981. Paraphrase relationships among clefted sentences. In G. D. Prideaux, B. L. Derwing & W. J. Baker (eds.), *Experimental Linguistics: Integration of Theories and Applications*. Ghent: Story-Scientia.

Foley, W. & Van Valin, R. 1977. On the viability of the notion of *subject* in universal grammar. *Proceedings of the 3rd Annual Meeting of the Berkeley Linguistics Society*, 293-320.

Foley, W. & Van Valin, R. 1985. Information packaging in the clause. In T. Shopen, *Language Typology and Syntactic Description*, Vol. 1, 282-364.

Cambridge: CUP.

Fox, B. A. 1987. The NP accessibility hierarchy reinterpreted: subject primacy or the absolute hypothesis? *Language* 63(4): 856-870.

Frajzyngier, Z. 1987. From preposition to copula. In D. Odden (ed.), *Current Approaches to African Linguistics*, *IV*, 371-86. Dordrecht: Foris.

Fries, P. H. 1981. On the status of theme in English. *Forum Linguisticum* 6(1): 1-38.

Gao, Q. 1995. The syntactic structure of Chinese formal focus. *Working Papers in Linguistics* 47: 21-46. Columbus, Oh (Wpl).

Gawron, J. M. 1986. Clefts, discourse representations, and situation semantics. In V. Nikiforidou, M. VanClay, M. Niepokuj & D. Feder (eds.). *Proceedings of the Twelfth Annual Meeting of the Berkeley Linguistics Society*. Berkeley: Berkeley Linguistics Society.

Geluykens, R. 1988. Five types of clefting in English discourse. *Linguistics* 26(5): 823-41.

Geluykens, R. R. 1991. Discourse functions of it-clefts in English conversation. *Communication and Cognition* 24(3-4): 343-358.

Geluykens, R. 1992. *From Discourse Process to Grammatical Construction: On Left-Dislocation in English*. Philadelphia: John Benjamins.

Gil, D. 1984. On the notion of "direct object" in patient prominent languages. In F. Plank (ed.), *Objects*, 87-108. New york: Academic Press.

Gili, J. 1974. *Introductory Catalan Grammar*. Oxford: the Dolphin Book Co.

Givón, T. 1979. *On Understanding Grammar*. New York: Academic Press.

Givón, T. 1982. Tense-aspect-modality: the creole prototype and beyond. In P. Hopper (ed.), *Tense and Aspect: Between Semantics and Pragmatics*, *Typological Studies in Language*, Vol. 1, Amsterdam: John Benjamins.

Givón, T. (ed.) 1983. *Topic Continuity in Discourse: A Quantitative Crosslanguage Study* (Typological Studies in Language, 3). Amsterdam: John Benjamins.

Givón, T. 1984a. Direct object and dative shifting. In F. Plank (ed.), *Objects*, 151-182. New York: Academic Press.

Givón, T. 1984b. *Syntax I: A Functional-Typological Introduction*. Amsterdam: Benjamins Publishing Co.

Givón, T. 1985. Iconicity isomorphism and non-arbitrary coding in syntax. In J. Haiman 1985b, 187-219.

Givón, T. 1990. *Syntax II: A Functional-Typological Introduction.* Amsterdam: Benjamins Publishing Co.

Glinert, L. 1989. *The Grammar of Modern Hebrew.* Cambridge: Cambridge University Press.

Goldsmith, J. 1981. On Spanish pseudo-clefts. *Glossa* 15(1): 3-15.

Gragg, G. B. 1972. Cleft sentences in Tigrinya. *Journal of African Languages* 2 (2): 74-89.

Graham, A. C. 1967. *Being in* Classical Chinese. In J. Verhaar (ed.), *The Verb "Be" and its Synonyms*, Vol. 1, 1-39. Dordrecht: D. Reidel.

Greenberg, J. H. 1966. Some universals of grammar with particular reference to the order of meaningful elements. In J. H. Greenberg (ed.), *Universals of Language*, 58-90. Cambridge, Mass.: MIT Press.

Greenberg, J. H. 1985. Some iconic relationships among place, time and discourse deixis. In J. Haiman (ed.), *Iconicity in Syntax*, 271-87. Amsterdam: John Benjamins Publishing Co.

Gundel, J. K. 1977. Where do cleft sentences come from? *Language* 53(3): 543-559.

Gundel, J. K. 1985. "Shared knowledge" and topicality. *Journal of Pragmatics* 9: 83-107.

Haig, J. H. 1982. Particle retention in predicated and cleft sentences. *Journal of the Association of Teachers of Japanese* 16(1): 7-29.

Hailu, H. F. 1985. Cleft constructions. *Studies in African Linguistics*, supp. 9: 128-34.

Haiman, J. 1974. *Targets and Syntactic Change.* The Hague: Mouton.

Haiman, J. 1985a. *Natural Syntax.* Cambridge: Cambridge University Press.

Haiman, J. (ed.). 1985b. *Iconicity in Syntax.* Amsterdam: John Benjamins.

Haiman, J. 1988. Incorporation, parallelism, and focus. In Hammond et al. 1988, 303-320.

Haiman, J. 1991. Motivation, repetition and emancipation: the bureaucratization of language. In H. C. Wolfart (ed.), *Linguistic Studies Presented to John L. Finley*, 45-70. Memoire 8, Algonquian and Iroquoian Linguistics. Winnipeg, Manitoba.

Haiman, J. 1993. Asserted Identity. Ms., Macalester College.

Haiman, J. 1995. Moods and metamessages: alienation as a mood. In J. Bybee &

S. Fleischmann (eds.), *Modality in Grammar and Discourse*, 329-345. Amsterdam: John Benjamins.

Halliday, M. A. K. 1967. Notes on transitivity and theme in English. (Part 2). *Journal of Linguistics* 3: 199-244.

Halliday, M. A. K. 1968. Notes on transitivity and theme in English. (Part 3). *Journal of Linguistics* 4: 153-308.

Halliday, M. A. K. 1970. Language structure and language function. In J. Lyons (ed.), *New Horizons in Linguistics*, 140-165. Harmondsworth: Penguin.

Halliday, M. A. K. 1976. Notes on transitivity and theme in English. (Part 2). *Journal of Linguistics* 3: 199-244.

Halliday, M. A. K. 1985. *An Introduction to Functional Grammar*. London: Edward Arnold.

Halvorsen, P-K. 1976. Syntax and semantics of cleft-sentences. *Papers from the* 12*th Regional Meeting*, CLS. Chicago: CLS.

Hammond, M., Moravcsik, E. & Wirth, J. (eds.) 1988. *Studies in Syntactic Typology*. Philadelphia: John Benjamins.

Hankamer, J. 1974. On the non-cyclic nature of WH-clefting. *Papers from the* 10*th Regional Meeting of the Chicago Linguistic Society*, 221-232. University of Chicago: Chicago Linguistic Society.

Harbour, D. 2008. Predicate clefts in Haitian. *Lingua* 118(7): 853-871.

Harries-Delisle, H. 1978. Contrastive emphasis and cleft sentences. In J. H. Greenberg (ed.), *Universals of Human Languages*, Vol. 4, 419-86. Stanford, California: Stanford University Press.

Harrison, S. P. 1976. *Mokilese Reference Grammar*. Honolulu: The University Press of Hawaii.

Harvard-Yenching Institute Sinologicaly Index Series, supplement No. 20: *A Concordance to Chuang Tzu*. Taipei: Chinese Materials & Research Aids Service Centre, Inc. 1966.

Hashimoto, A. Y. 1969. The verb "to be" in modern Chinese. In J. W. M. Verhaar (ed.), *The Verb "Be" and Its Synonyms*, Vol. 9, 72-111. Dordrecht: D. Reidel Publishing Co.

Hauenscild, C. 1982. Demonstrative pronouns in Russian and Czech: deixis and anaphora. In J. Weissenborn & W. Klein (eds.), *Here and There: Crosslinguistic Studies on Deixis and Demonstration*, 167-196. Amsterdam: John

Benjamins.

Hawkins, J. A. (ed.) 1988a. *Explaining Language* Universals. Oxford: Basil Blackwell.

Hawkins, J. A. 1988b. Explaining language universals. In J. A. Hawkins 1988a, 3-30. Oxford: Basil Blackwell.

Hedberg, N. 2006. Topic-focus controversies. In Valeria Molnar and Susanne Winkler (eds.), *The Architecture of Focus*, 1-25. Mouton de Gruyter.

Hedberg, N. 2000. The Referential Status of Clefts, *Language* 76: 891-920.

Heggie, L. A. 1988. *The Syntax of Copular Sentences.* Doctoral dissertation, Los Angeles: University of Southern California.

Hengeveld, K. 1990. A functional analysis of copula constructions in Mandarin Chinese. *Studies in Language* 14: 291-323.

Herring, S. & Paolillo, J. 1995. Focus position in SOV languages. In P. Downing & M. Noonan (eds.), *Word Order in Discourse* (Typological Studies in Language 30), 163-198. Amsterdam: John Benjamins.

Higgins, F. R. 1976. *The Pseudo-Cleft Construction in English.* Indiana University Linguistics Club.

Hirakouji, K. 1982. On deriving pseudo-cleft sentences from cleft sentences. *Journal of the English Institute* 5: 67-93.

Hoekstra, T., van der Hulst, H. & Moortgat, M. (eds.) 1981. *Perspectives on Functional Grammar.* Dordrecht: Foris.

Hoffmann, C. 1963. *A Grammar of the Margi Language.* London: Oxford University Press.

Horn, L. R. 1981. Exhaustiveness and the semantics of clefts. In V. Burk & J. Pustejovsky (eds.), *Proceedings of the* 11*th Annual Meeting of the North Eastern Linguistic Society*, 125-42. Amherst: University of Massachusetts.

Houng, C. C-L H. 1986. *The Relative Clause Construction in Chinese: NP Accessibility and Other Issues.* Doctoral dissertation, University of Texas at Austin.

Hsueh, F. 1983. A note on the grammatical function of gei. *Journal of Chinese Language Teachers Association* 14:81-85.

Huang, C-T. J. 1982a. Move WH in a language without WH movement. *Linguistic Review* 1(4): 369-416.

Huang, C-T. 1982b. *Logical Relations in Chinese and the Theory of Grammar.* Ph.

D. dissertation, MIT.

Huang, C-T. 1988. *Wo pao de kuai* and Chinese phrase structure. *Language* 64 (2): 274-311.

Huddleston, R. 1984. *Introduction to the Grammar of English.* Cambridge: Cambridge University Press.

Huang, C-T. 1988. *English Grammar: An Outline.* Cambridge: CUP.

Hupet, M. & Tilmant, B. 1986. What are clefts good for? Some consequences for comprehension. *Journal of Memory and Language* 25: 419-430.

Jackendoff, R. 1972. *Semantic Interpretation in Generative Grammar.* Cambridge, Mass.: The MIT Press.

Jackendoff, R. 1983. *Semantics and Cognition.* Cambridge, Mass.: The MIT Press.

Jensen, J. T. 1977. *Yapese Reference Grammar.* Honolulu: University Press of Hawaii.

Jespersen, O. 1949. *A Modern English Grammar.* Vol. II, (Part 4). Heidelberg, (originally published in 1909).

Jespersen, O. 1961. *A Modern Grammar on Historical Principles, Part VII, syntax.* London: Allen and Unwin.

Johnson, D. E. 1974. *Toward a Theory of Relationally-Based Grammar.* Doctoral dissertation, University of Illinois, Urbana, Illinois.

Jones, L. B. & Jones, L. K. 1985. Discourse functions of five English sentence types. *Word* 36(1): 1-21.

Kamio, A. 1991. Cleft sentences and the territory of information. In C. Georgopolous & R. Ishihara (eds.), *Interdisciplinary Approaches to Language: Essays in Honor of S. -Y.* Kuroda. Dordrecht: Kluwer, 353-371.

Kang, B. 2006. Some peculiarities of Korean *kes* cleft constructions. *Studia Linguistica*, 60(3): 251-281.

Keenan, E. L. 1972. Relative clause formation in Malagasy. In P. M. Peranteau, J. N. Levi & G. C. Phares (eds.), *The Chicago Which Hunt: Papers from the Relative Clause Festival*, 169-89. Chicago: Chicago Linguistic Society.

Keenan, E. L. 1987a. *Universal Grammar: 15 Essays.* London: Croom Helm.

Keenan, E. L. 1987b. Variation in universal grammar. In Keenan 1987a, 46-59.

Keenan, E. L. 1987c. Towards a universal definition of subject of. in Keenan 1987a, 89-120.

Keenan, E. & Comrie, B. 1977. Noun phrase accessibility and universal grammar. *Linguistic Inquiry* 8(1): 63-99.

Keenan, E. & Comrie, B. 1979a. Noun phrase accessibility revisited. *Language* 55: 649-64.

Keenan, E. & Comrie, B. 1979b. Data on the noun phrase accessibility hierarchy. *Language* 55: 333-351.

Keenan, E. & Gary J. O. 1987. On collapsing grammatical relations in universal grammar. In Keenan 1987a, 121-65.

Keenan, E. & Hawkins, Sarah. 1987. The psychological validity of the Accessibility Hierarchy. In Keenan 1987a, 60-85. London: Croom Helm.

Keenan, E. & Hull, R. 1973. The logical syntax and direct and indirect questions. *CIS Parasession on Subordination*, 348-370.

Kimenyi, A. 1978. *A Relational Grammar of Kinyarwanda.* Berkeley: University of California Press.

Kiss, K. E. 1977. The notion of topic and focus. *Hungarian Studies in English* 11: 211-23.

Knowles, J. 1986. The cleft sentence: a base-generated perspective. *Lingua* 69 (4): 295-317.

Koch, J. T. 1985. Movement and emphasis in the Gaulish sentence. *The Bulletin of the Board of Celtic Studies*, Vol. 32: 1-37.

König, E. 1991. *The Meaning of Focus Particles: A Comparative Perspective.* London: Routledge.

Koopman, H. 1984. *The Syntax of Verbs.* Dordrecht: Foris.

Koopman, W. et al. (eds.) 1987. *Explanation and Linguistic Change.* Current Issues in Linguistic Theory, Vol. 45. Amsterdam: John Benjamins Publishing Co.

Langacker, R. & Monro, P. 1975. Passives and their meaning. *Language* 51: 789-830.

Langendoen, D. T. 1980. The accessibility of deep structure. In R. A. Jacobs and P. S. Rosenbaum (ed.), *Readings in English Transformational Grammar*, 99-104.

Larsen, T. W. 1981. Functional correlates of ergativity in Aguacatec. In D. Alford et al. (eds.), *Proceedings of the Seventh Annual Meeting of the Berkeley Linguistic Society*, 136-53. Berkeley: Berkeley Linguistics Society.

Larsen, T. W. & Norman, W. M. 1979. Correlates of ergativity in Mayan grammar. In F. Plank (ed.), *Ergativity*, 347-370. London: Academic Press.

Law, P. 2007. The syntactic structure of the cleft construction in Malagasy. *Nat Lang Linguist Theory*, 25: 765-823.

Leap, W. L. 1980. Cleft and pseudo-cleft in Tewa English. In F. Barkin & E. Brandt (eds.), *Speaking, Singing and Teaching: A Multidisciplinary Approach to Language Variation*, 179-91. Tempe: Arizona State University.

Lee, K-D. 1975. *Kusaiean Reference Grammar.* Honolulu: The University Press of Hawaii.

Lee, K-D. 1976. *Kusaiean-English Dictionary.* Honolulu: The University Press of Hawaii.

Lee, M. 1988. Language, perception and the world. In J. Hawkins 1988a, 211-46. Oxford: Basil Blackwell.

Leech, G. and Svartvik, J. 1975. *A Communicative Grammar of English.* London: Longman.

Lees, R. B. 1963. Analysis of the "cleft sentence" in English. *Zeitschrift für Phonetik, Sprachwissenschaft und Kommuunikationsforschung* 16: 371-388.

Lefebvre, C. 1992. Towards a typology of predicate cleft languages. *Journal of West African Languages*, 22(1): 53-61.

Lehmann, C. 1986. On the typology of relative clauses. *Linguistics* 24: 663-80.

Lempert, H. 1984. *Topic as Starting Point for Syntax.* Monographs of the Society for Research in Child Development, serial No. 208, v. 49, No. 5., published by the University of Chicago Press.

Lewis, C. 1971. *Alice in Wonderland.* Oxford: Oxford University Press.

Li, C. (ed.) 1976. *Subject and Topic.* New York: Academic Press.

Li, C. & Thompson, S. 1974. Co-verbs in Mandarin Chinese: verbs or prepositions? *Journal of Chinese Linguistics* 2: 257-278.

Li, C. & Thompson, S. 1974. An explanation of word order change SVO-SOV. *Foundations of Language* 12: 201-214.

Li, C. & Thompson, S. 1975. A mechanism for the development of copula morpheme. In C. Li (ed.), *Word Order and Word Order Change*, 419-44. Austin: University of Texas Press.

Li, C. & Thompson, S. 1975. The semantic function of word order: a case study in Mandarin. In Charles N. Li (ed.). *Word Order and Word Order Change*, 163-

95. Austin: University of Texas Press.

Li, C. & Thompson, S. 1981. *Mandarin Chinese: A Functional Reference Grammar.* Berkeley: University of California Press.

Li, Y-H A. 1990. *Order and Constituency in Mandarin Chinese.* Dordrecht: Kluwer Academic Publishers.

Lightfoot, D. W. 1979. *Principles of Diachronic Syntax.* Cambridge: Cambridge University Press.

Lin, H. T. 1981. *Essential Grammar for Modern Chinese.* Boston: Cheng & Tsui.

Liu, B. 1987. Clearing the mist of Chang'an. In his *Self-Selected Anthology of Liu Bingyan.* Hongkong: Cosmos Books Ltd.

Lumsden, J. S. & Lefebvre, C. 1990. Predicate-cleft constructions and why they aren't what you might think. *Linguistics* 28(4): 761-782.

Luo, C. 1992. On the uncleftability of direct object in Chinese. *Linguistica Atlantica* 14: 55-71.

Luo, C. 1993. The Accessibility Hierarchy and clefting: a crosslinguistic perspective. In M. Bernstein (ed.), *Proceedings of the 9th Eastern States Conference on Linguistics*, 184-195. Ithaca: Cornell University.

Luo, C. 1994a. Grammatical relations, transitivity and ergativity: an interactive view of cleftability. *Linguistica Atlantica*, 16: 85-102.

Luo, C. 1994b. Thematicity and cleftability. In D. Jory & V. Motapanyane (eds.), *Papers from the Eighteenth Annual Meeting of the Atlantic Provinces Linguistic Association.* University of New Brunswick, Sait John, N. B.: Atlantic Provinces Linguistic Association, 54-73.

Maxwell, D. N. 1979. Strategies of relativization and NP accessibility. *Language* 55: 352-71.

McCloskey, J. 1979. *Transformational Syntax and Model Theoretical Semantics.* Dordrecht: D. Reidel Publishing Co.

McWhorter, J. 1994. From focus marker to copula in Swahili. In K. Moore, D. Peterson & W. Comfort (eds.), *Proceedings of the 20t Annual Meeting of the Berkeley Linguistic Society*, 57-66. Berkeley: Berkeley Linguistic Society.

Mey, J. 1993. *Pragmatics: an Introduction.* Oxford: Blackwell.

Modini, P. 1993. A theory of evolution of the Mandarin focus construction "shi... de". *Asian and African Studies*, 154-168.

Mohanan, K. P. 1982. Grammatical relations and clause structure in Malayalam. In

Bresnan 1982: 504-89.

Moriguchi, T. 1995. Subject and focus in Philippine-Formosan native languages. *Journal of the Linguistic Society of Japan*, 107: 87-112. Kyoto, Japan.

Nemer, J. F. 1987. Negation and clefting in Temne. In D. Odden (ed.). *Current Approaches to African Linguistics*, *IV*, 281-299. Dordrecht: Foris.

Newmeyer, R. J. 1992. Iconicity and generative grammar. *Language* 68(4): 756-796.

Newman, P. 1970. *A Grammar of Tera*. Berkeley: University of California Press.

Nolke, H. 1984. Clefting in Danish? *Nydanske Studier and Almen Kommunikationsteori* 14: 72-111.

Nylander, D. K. 1985. A new analysis of the Krio cleft predicate. *Studies in African Linguistics*. Dec.; supp. 9: 251-253.

Oehrle, R. T. 1983. The inaccessibility of the inner NP: corrections and speculations. *Linguistic Analysis* 12(2): 159-71.

Partee B. H. 1979. *Subject and Object in Modern English*. New York: Garland Publishing, Inc.

Pavesi, M. 1986. Markedness, discourse modes, and relative clause ... *Studies in Second Language Acquisition* 8(1): 38-55.

Pawley, A. K. 1966. Polynesian languages: a subgrouping based on shared innovations in morphology. *Journal of the Polynesian Society* 75: 39-64.

Perlmutter, D. M. & Postal, P. M. 1974. Some general laws of grammar. Mimeo.

Percival, W. K. 1981. *A Grammar of the Urbanised Toba-Batak of Medan*. Pacific Linguistic Series B, No. 76. Australian National University.

Pinkham, J. & Hankamer, J. 1975. Deep and shallow clefts. *Papers from the* 11*th Regional Meeting of the Chicago Linguistic Society*, 429-450. Chicago: CLS, University of Chicago.

Plank, F. 1979. *Ergativity*. New York: Academic Press.

Plank, F. 1984. *Objects: Towards a Theory of Grammatical Relations*. New York: Academic Press.

Plank, F. 1985. *Relational Typology*. Berlin: Mouton.

Prince, E. F. 1978. A comparison of WH-clefts and it-clefts in discourse. *Language* 54(4): 883-906.

Pullum, G. K. 1977. Word order universals and grammatical relations. In P. Cole & J. M. Sadock (eds.). *Syntax and Semantics* Vol. 8, 249-77. New York:

Academic Press.

Quirk, R. et al. 1985. *A Comprehensive Grammar of the English Language.* London: Longman.

Radford, A. 1979. The functional basis of transformations. *Transactions of the Philological Society*: 1-42.

Radford, A. 1981. *Transformational Syntax.* Cambridge: Cambridge University Press.

Reid, L. A. 1966. *An Ivatan Syntax.* Oceanic Linguistics, special publication No. 2. Hanululu: the Pacific and Asian Linguistics Institute, University of Hawaii.

Reimer, M. 1992. Three views of demonstrative reference. *Synthese* 93: 373-402.

Reinhart, T. 1980. On the position of extraposed clauses. *Linguistic Inquiry* 11(3): 621-24.

Reinhart, T. 1982. *Pragmatics and Linguistics: An Analysis of Sentence Topics.* Bloomington, Indiana: Indiana University Linguistics Club.

Ritchie, W. C. (ed.) 1978. *Second Language Acquisition Research: Issues and Implications.* New York: Academic Press.

Robinson, J. O. 1972. Focus, presuppoisition and WH-questions in Igbo. Paper presented at the Third Conference on African Linguistics, Bloomington.

Rochemont, M. S. & Culicover, P. W. 1990. *English Focus Construction and the Theory of Grammar.* Cambridge: Cambridge University Press.

Ross, C. 1983. On the function of Mandarin DE. *Journal of Chinese Linguistics* 11 (2): 214-246.

Ross, J. 1967. Constraints on variables in syntax. Ph. D. thesis, MIT.

Saltarelli, M. 1988. *Basque.* London: Croom Helm.

Sandmann, M. 1979 (2nd ed.). *Subject and Predicate: A Contribution to the Theory of Syntax.* Heidelberg: Carl Winter Universitätsverlag.

Sanford, A. J., Moar, K. & Garrod, S. C. 1988. Proper names as controllers of discourse focus. *Language and Speech* 31(1): 43-56.

Saul, J. E. & Wilson, N. F. 1980. *Nung Grammar. Dallas*, Texas: Summer Institute of Linguistics.

Schachter, P. 1973. Focus and relativization. *Language* 49: 19-46.

Schachter, P. 1976. The subject in Philippine languages: topic, actor, actor-topic, or none of the above? In C. Li (ed.), *Subject and Topic*, 491-518. New York: Academic Press.

Schachter, P. 1977. Reference-related and role-related properties of subjects. In P. Cole et al. (eds.), *Syntax and Semantics 8: Grammatical Relations*, 279-306. New York: Academic Press.

Schuh, R. G. 1971. Reconstruction of the syntax of subject emphasis in certain Chadic languages. *Studies in African Linguistics*, *Supplement* 2: 67-77.

Sebeok, T. 1994. *Signs: an Introduction to Semiotics.* Toronto: University of Toronto Press.

Sgall, P., Hajicová, E. & Benesová, E. 1973. *Topic, Focus and Generative Semantics.* Kronberg: Scriptor Verlag.

Shaumyan, S. 1985. Ergativity and universal grammar. In F. Plank (ed.), *Relational Typology*, 311-338. Berlin: Mouton.

Shibatani, M. 1988 (ed.). *Passive and Voice.* Amsterdam: John Benjamins.

Shopen, T. 1985. *Language Typology and Syntactic Description*, Vol. 1-3. Cambridge: CUP.

Sigurd, B. 1989. A supplementary relativization hierarchy based on the complexity of the relative phrase. *Studia Linguistica* 43(1): 33-46.

Simons, P. 1982. Ne... ba marking in Lele: a cleft construction? *Studies in African Linguistics* 13: 217-229.

Smits, R. J. C. 1989. *Eurogrammar: the Relative and Cleft Constructions of the Germanic and Romance Languages.* Dordrecht: Foris.

Sornicola, R. 1988. It-clefts and wh-clefts: two awkward sentence types. *Journal of Linguistics* 24(2): 343-379.

Spaulding, R. K. 1959. *Syntax of the Spanish Verb.* New York: Holt, Rinehart & Winston.

Steed, J. 1993. In pursuit of power: Kim Campbell: a portrait. In *The Toronto Star*, May 1, 1993, D1-D6.

Stein, D. 1988. Semantic similarity between categories as a vehicle of linguistic change. *Diachronica* V: 1/2: 1-19.

Stenson, N. 1979. Questions on the accessibility hierarchy. In P. R. Clyne, Hanks & Hofbauer (eds.). *The Elements: A Parasession on Linguistic Units and Levels*, 248-259. Chicago: CLS.

Suarez, J. A. 1983. *The Mesoamerican Indian Languages.* Cambridge: Cambridge Language Surveys.

Sun, C. & Givón, T. 1985. On the so-called SOV word order in Mandarin Chinese:

a quantitative text study and its implications. *Language* 61(2): 329-351.

Taglicht, J. 1984. *Message and Emphasis: On Focus and Scope in English.* London: Longman.

Tai, J. 1973, Chinese as a SOV language. *Papers from the Ninth Regional Meeting of Chicago Linguistic Society*, 659-671. Chicago: CLS, University of Chicago.

Tai, J. 1976. Semantics and syntax of "inner" and "outer" locatives. *Proceedings of 1976 Mid-America Linguistics Conference*, 301-310. Minnesota: Linguistics Department: University of Minnesota.

Takizala, A. 1973. Focus and relativization: the case of Kihung'an. In J. P. Kimball (ed.), *Syntax and Semantics*, Vol. 2, 123-148. New York: Seminar Press.

Tallerman, M. 1990. Relativization strategies: NP accessibility in Welsh. *Journal of Linguistics* 26: 291-314.

Tchekjoff, C. 1979. From ergative to accusative in Tongan: an example of synchronic dynamics. In F. Plank (ed.), *Ergativity*, 407-418. New York: Academic Press.

Teng, S-H. 1979. Remarks on cleft sentences in chinese. *Journal of Chinese Linguistics*, 7: 101-114.

Tiee, H. H-Y. 1986. *A Reference Grammar of Chinese Sentences.* Tucson: University of Arizona Press.

Thompson, S. & Longacre, R. 1985. Adverbial clauses. In T. Shopen (ed.), *Language Typology and Syntactic Description*, Vol. II., 171-234. Cambridge: Cambridge University Press.

Timm, L. A. 1987. Cleft structures in Breton. *Word* 38(2): 127-142.

Tobin, Y. 1995. The iconicity of focus and existence in Modern Hebrew. In M. Landsberg (ed.), *Syntactic Iconicity and Linguistic Freezes: the Human Dimension* (Studies in Anthropological Linguistics 9), 177-188. Berlin: Mouton De Gruyter.

Tomlin, Russel 1985. Interaction of subject, theme, and agent. In J. R. Wirth (ed.), 1985. *Beyond the Sentence: Discourse and Sentential Form.* Ann Arbor: Karoma Publishers, Inc.

Travis, L. 1984. *Parameters and Effects of Word Order Variation.* Unpublished Ph. D. dissertation, MIT.

Trithart, L. 1975. Relational grammar and Chichewa subjectivisation rules. In R. E.

Crossman, L. J. Sam, and T. J. Vance (eds.), *Papers from the Eleventh Regional Meeting of the Chicago Linguistic Society*, University of Chicago, Chicago, Illinois.

Trithart, L. 1977. *Relational Grammar and Chichewa Subjectivization Rules.* Bloomington, Indiana University Linguistics Club.

Urogdi, B. 2006. Predicate Fronting and Dative Case in Hungarian. *Acta Linguistica Hungarica*, 53(3): 291-332.

Van Dijk, T. A. 1977. Sentence topic and discourse topic. *Papers in Slavic Philology* 1: 49-61.

Van Gelderen, E. 1991. "To be" and indices. In W. Abraham, W. Kosmeijer & E. Reuland (eds.), *Issues in Germanic Syntax*, 307-325. Berlin: Mouton De Gruyter.

Vion, M. & Colas, A. 1995. Contrastive marking in French dialogue: why and how. *Journal of Psycholinguistic Research*, 24(5): 313-331.

Van Riemsdijk, H. C. 1978. *A Case in Syntactic Markedness: Binding Nature of PP.* Lisse: Ridder.

Verhaar, J. W. M. (ed.) 1969. *The Verb 'Be' and Its Synonyms*, Vol. 9. Dordrecht: D. Reidel Publishing Co.

Von der Tuuk, H. N. 1971. *A Grammar of Toba Batak.* The Hague: Martinus Nijhoff.

Wang, L. 1984. *Wang Li Wen Ji* (Works of Wang Li), *Vol. 1.* Jinan: Shandong Jiaoyu Chubanshe.

Wang, L. 1985. *Modern Chinese Grammar.* Beijing: Commercial Press.

Wang, R. 1990. The hunger trilogy. In his *The Second Marriage.* Taibei: Lin Bai Press Ltd.

Weinert, R. 1995. Focusing constructions in spoken language: clefts, Y-movement, thematization and deixis in English and German. *Linguistische Berichte*, 159: 341-369.

Welmers, W. E. 1964. The syntax of emphasis in Kpelle. *The Journal of West African Languages* 1(1): 13-26.

Werth, P. 1979. If linear order isn't in the base ... the role of focus in word-order. In J. M. Meisel & D. P. Martin (eds.), *Linear Order and Generative Theory.* (Current Issues in Linguistic Theory 7). Amsterdam: Benjamins.

Werth, P. 1984. *Focus, Coherence and Emphasis.* London: Croom Helm.

Wirth, J. R. 1978. The derivation of cleft sentences in English. *Glossa* 12(1): 58-82.

Wirth, Jessica R. (ed.) 1985. *Beyond the Sentence: Discourse and Sentential Form.* Ann Arbor: Karoma Publishers, Inc.

Wolvengrey, A. 1990. A marker of contrastive focus in Mandan. Ms., University of Manitoba.

Woolford, E. 1978. Topicalization and clefting without WH-movement. In M. J. Stein (ed.), *Papers from the Eighth Annual Meeting of the North Eastern Linguistic Society.* University of Massachusetts at Amherst, Mass.

Yen, S. 1986. The origin of the copula *shi* in Chinese. *Journal of Chinese Linguistics* 14: 227-242.

Zhou, Z. et al. 1982. *Han Fei Zi Suoying* (An Index to Han Fei Zi). Beijing: Zhonghua Shu Ju.

Zubin, D. A. & Li, N. 1986. Topic, contrast, definiteness, and word order in Mandarin. In V. Nikiforidou *et al.* (eds.), *Proceedings of the 12th Annual Meeting of the Berkeley Linguistics Society*, 292-304. Berkeley: Berkeley Linguistics Society.

Language Index

Subject Index